1992

Science for Kids
39 EASY
GEOGRAPHY ACTIVITIES

Science For Kids
39 EASY
GEOGRAPHY ACTIVITIES

Robert W. Wood
Illustrated by John D. Wood

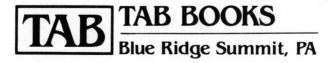
TAB BOOKS
Blue Ridge Summit, PA

FIRST EDITION
FIRST PRINTING

© 1992 by **TAB Books**.
TAB Books is a division of McGraw-Hill, Inc.

Library of Congress Cataloging-in-Publication Data

Wood, Robert W., 1933 –
    Science for kids : 39 easy geography activities / by Robert W.
Wood.
      p.   cm.
    Includes index.
    Summary: Introduces the science of geography through thirty-nine
activities, including ''Finding North by the Sun,'' ''Making a
Compass,'' and ''Neighborhood Research.''
    ISBN 0-8306-2493-7 (hard)   ISBN 0-8306-2492-9 (pbk.) :
    1. Geography—Experiments—Juvenile literature. [1. Geography—
Experiments. 2. Experiments.]   I. Title.
G74.W66 1991
910—dc20   91-23911
                                                  CIP
                                                    AC

TAB Books offers software for sale. For information and a catalog, please contact TAB Software Department, Blue Ridge Summit, PA 17294-0850.

Acquisitions Editor: Kimberly Tabor
Book Editor: Susan L. Rockwell
Production: Katherine G. Brown
Book Design: Jaclyn J. Boone
Cover photo: Susan Riley, Harrisonburg, VA

SFK

Contents

Introduction

The Science for Kids series consists of eight books introducing astronomy, chemistry, meteorology, geology, engineering, plant biology, animal biology, and geography.

Science is a subject that becomes instantly exciting with even simple discoveries. On any day, and at any time, we can see these mysteries unfold around us.

The series was written to open the door and invite the curious to enter—to explore, to think, and to wonder. To realize that anyone, absolutely anyone at all, can experiment and learn. To discover that the only thing you really need to study science is an inquiring mind. The rest of the material is all around you. It is there for anyone to see. You have only to look.

This book, *39 Easy Geography Activities*, is the eighth in the Science for Kids series. The word *geography* comes to us from the Greek word *geographia*, which means earth description. Geography is the descriptive science that deals with the surface of the earth and how the earth is divided into continents. It is a study of people, plants, and animals, and where they are located on a map, and just as important, why things are located in a particular place.

People have always had a need for geographic knowledge. Early humans had to find shelter in caves. They needed a regular supply of water and a place to hunt. Their daily lives depended on the weather, and the gathering of wild seeds and fruits depended on the seasons. These early people used colored clay or charred sticks to draw maps of their surroundings on the walls of their caves and on the dried skins of animals. However, their geographic knowledge probably did not extend much past a day's travel.

Today, we cannot be content with just knowing the geography of our neighborhoods. We must know something about the geography of the entire world. Newspapers and television are full of stories about the happenings of people and places in distant lands. It would be impossible for us to understand what they are talking about without a fundamental understanding of geography. With today's communication and transportation, we find our world is not nearly as big as we thought. Although people around the world have different cultures, we all have one thing in common, we all live on the same earth.

The study of geography can lead to an interesting career in planning, research, or teaching. But, exciting careers are also available in associated fields such as surveying and mapping, geology, meteorology, and environmental management. The following experiments will help introduce this fascinating science.

Symbols Used in This Book

Some of the experiments used in this book require the use of sharp objects, hot water, and electricity. It is recommended that a parent or teacher supervise young children and instruct them.

All of the experiments in this book can be done safely, but young children should be instructed about the hazards associated with carelessness. The following symbols are used throughout the book for you to use as a guide to what children might be able to do independently, and what they *should not do* without adult supervision. Keep in mind that some children might not be mature enough to do some of the experiments without adult help, and that these symbols should be used as a guide only and do not replace good judgment of parents or teachers.

 Materials or tools used in this experiment could be dangerous in young hands. Adult supervision is recommended. Children should be instructed on the care and handling of sharp tools or combustible or toxic materials and how to protect surfaces.

 The use of the stove, boiling water, or other hot materials are used in this project and adult supervision is required. Keep other small children away from boiling water and burners.

 Electricity is used in this experiment. Young children should be supervised and older children cautioned about the hazards of electricity.

1
Map of the Earth

Look at the map of the earth and you will notice that the North Pole is at the top and the South Pole is at the bottom (Fig. 1-1). You also can see that it is divided in the middle by the equator (Fig. 1-2). The map is further divided by lines running up and down and lines running from left to right, or around the globe. Map makers draw these lines to help us find directions, the time, and the seasons. The lines running up and down all come together at the North Pole and the South Pole. These are the lines of longitude (Fig. 1-3). The lines running across the map from left to right are the lines of latitude (Fig. 1-4). They are divided by the equator. The areas of the earth north of the equator have winter in January and summer in July. The areas south of the equator have opposite seasons—winter in July and summer in January (Fig. 1-5).

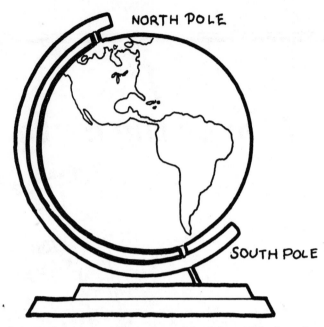

Fig. 1-1. *A globe is a spherical model of the earth that shows the continents and the seas.*

Fig 1-2. *The earth is divided around the middle by the equator.*

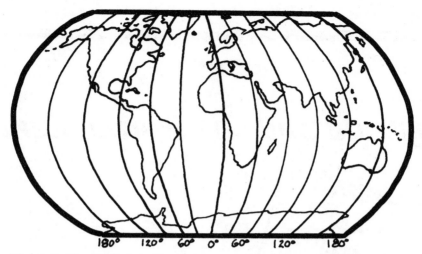

Fig. 1-3. *The lines that run from the North Pole to the South Pole are the lines of longitude.*

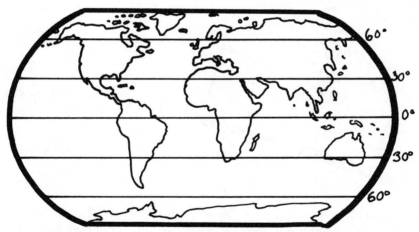

Fig. 1-4. *The lines that run from east to west are the lines of latitude.*

Fig. 1-5. *The areas that are divided by the equator have opposite seasons.*

2

Longitude and the Prime Meridian

Materials

- MAP OR GLOBE
- WATCH
- 2 STRAIGHT STICKS (ABOUT 12 INCHES LONG)
- HAMMER
- MAGNETIC COMPASS

Examine the map and locate the lines of longitude (Fig. 2-1). Find the 0 degree longitude line. It runs through Greenwich Observatory, near London (Fig. 2-2). This observatory marks the prime meridian of the earth. World time is calculated from this point. It is measured at the instant the sun passes directly over the observatory. Locations can be found by counting the longitude east and west from this imaginary line. The distance between the degrees becomes smaller as the lines of longitude approach the North Pole. For example, 1 degree longitude along the southern United States is about 60 miles wide, while 1 degree longitude across southern Canada is less than 45 miles wide (Fig. 2-3).

In a sunny area outside, and just before noon, draw a line in

4

the dirt running north and south (Fig. 2-4). Drive the two sticks straight into the ground on this line. Watch the shadows of both sticks (Fig. 2-5). When the two shadows are in line, the sun will be passing through its highest point (Fig. 2-6). This is the meridian, or longitude, of your location.

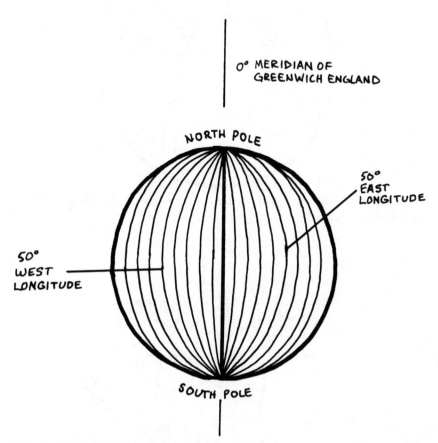

Fig. 2-1. *The lines of longitude are measured east and west from the 0 degree longitude line.*

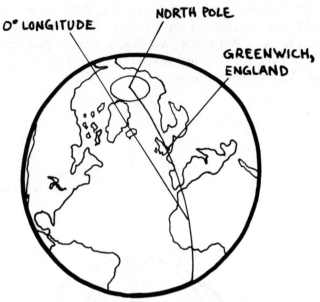

Fig. 2-2. *The 0 degree longitude lines, or prime median, runs through Greenwich, England.*

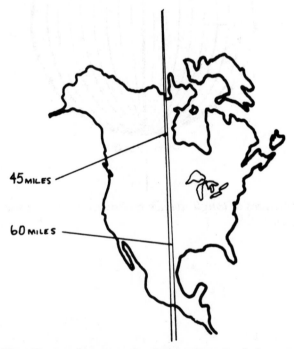

Fig. 2-3. *The distance between the degrees longitude becomes smaller as they approach the North and South Poles.*

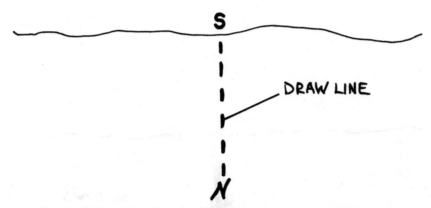

Fig. 2-4. *Scratch a line in the dirt that runs north and south.*

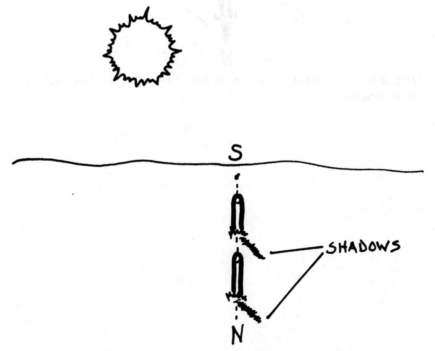

Fig. 2-5. *Notice the shadows that are created by the sticks.*

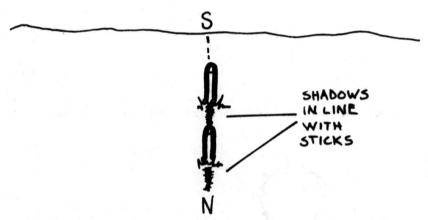

Fig. 2-6. *When the shadows are in line, they mark the longitude of your location.*

3
Finding North by the Sun

Drive the stick into the ground at an angle that points straight at the sun (Fig. 3-1). The stick should not make a shadow. Wait about an hour, or until the stick casts a shadow about 6 inches long. The shadow will be pointing east from the stick (Fig. 3-2). The sun has now moved toward the west. If you stand with your right shoulder pointing in the direction of the shadow (east), you will be facing north (Fig. 3-3).

Fig. 3-1. *Drive the stick into the ground at an angle directly at the sun.*

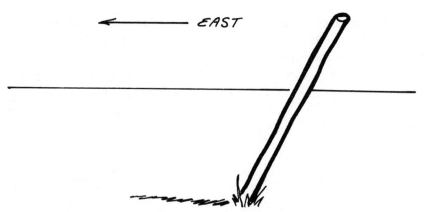

Fig. 3-2. *The stick will cast a shadow that points east.*

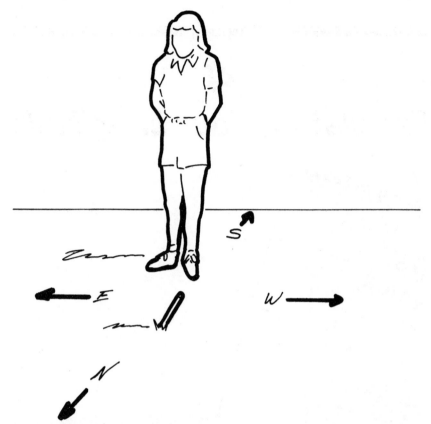

Fig. 3-3. *Point your right shoulder with the shadow and you will be facing north.*

4

Calculating Your Longitude

Materials

MAP
WATCH

Find the lines of longitude on the map. Locate the prime meridian, the 0 degree longitude line (Fig. 4-1).

There are 360 degrees in the earth's circumference. Because the earth turns once on its axis every 24 hours, 15 degrees of longitude pass beneath the sun each hour (Fig. 4-2). For each 15 degrees west of Greenwich, the time is set back one hour. For each 15 degrees east of Greenwich, the time is advanced one hour.

Find the line of longitude nearest your location. If you live along a line running from New Orleans north through St. Louis you might find a longitude of 90 degrees (Fig. 4-3). For example, the suburbs of Memphis lie across the 90 degree longitude line (Fig. 4-4). If you divide 90 degrees by 15 degrees, you can see that your location is about 6 hours from Greenwich. So if you know the Greenwich time (also called universal time or U.T.), and you know the time where you are, you can easily calculate your longitude. For example, if it is noon in Greenwich, and 6:00 AM where you are, you would have a longitude of 90 degrees west (Fig. 4-5).

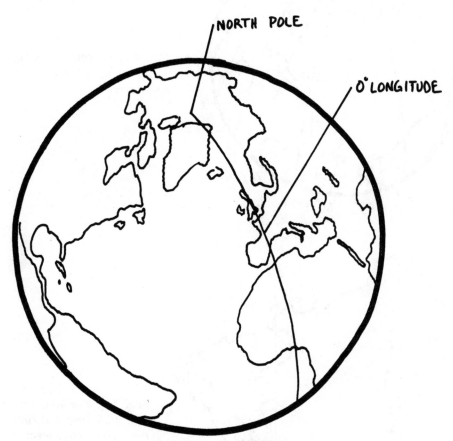

Fig. 4-1. *Find the prime median on the globe.*

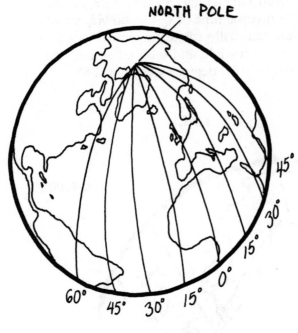

Fig. 4-2. *Fifteen degrees of longitude pass beneath the sun every hour.*

Fig. 4-3. *The 90 degree longitude line that runs through North America.*

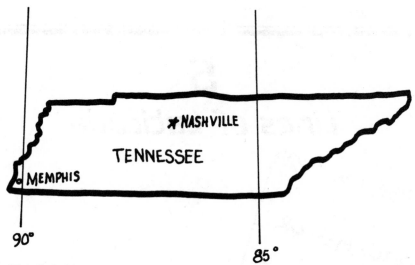

Fig. 4-4. *The 90 degree longitude line passes through the suburbs of Memphis, Tennessee.*

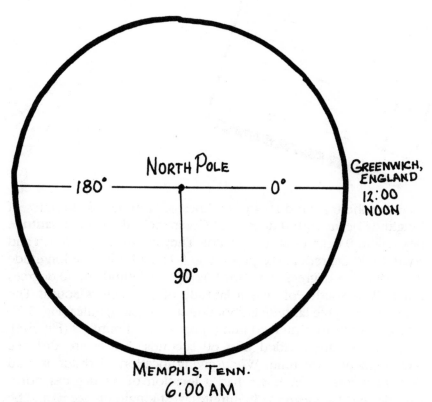

Fig. 4-5. *When it is twelve noon at Greenwich, England, it is 6:00 AM along the 90 degree line of longitude.*

5

Lines of Latitude

Examine the map and locate the lines of latitude. As the lines of longitude begin with 0 degrees at Greenwich, the lines of latitude begin with 0 degrees at the equator. They are measured north and south to 90 degrees at the poles (Fig. 5-1). Latitude, like longitude is measured in degrees. The North Pole has a latitude of 90 degrees north. The South Pole has a latitude of 90 degrees south. The length of 1 degree latitude is about 69 statute (land) miles (Fig. 5-2). Degrees are further divided into 60 parts called minutes (Fig. 5-3). The minutes are divided into 60 seconds. These are distance measurements, not time. When giving locations, latitude is read first, then longitude. If we had a location of 34 degrees north latitude, and 118 degrees, 30 minutes west longitude, we would be just off the beach of Santa Monica, California (Fig. 5-4).

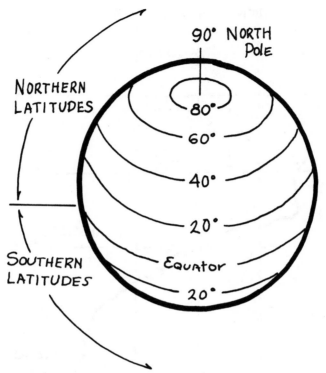

Fig. 5-1. *The lines of latitude are measured north and south from the equator.*

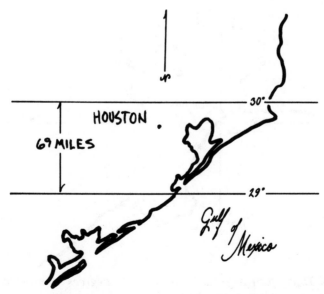

Fig. 5-2. *The length of 1 degree latitude is about 69 miles.*

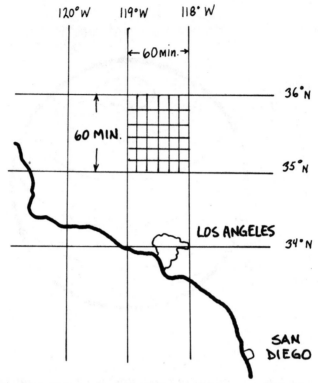

Fig. 5-3. *Degrees are divided into 60 parts called minutes.*

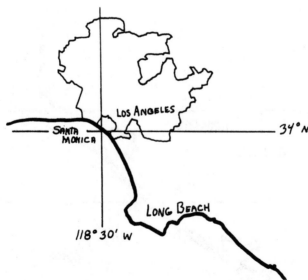

Fig. 5-4. *Thirty-four degrees north and 118 degrees 30 minutes west is a location near Santa Monica, California.*

6
Finding the North Star

Materials
- CLEAR NIGHT
- MAGNETIC COMPASS

The North Star is easy to find on a clear night. Simply face the northern half of the sky and locate the Big Dipper. The Big Dipper is a group of seven bright stars that look like the side view of a pan with a handle (Fig. 6-1). The Big Dipper moves in a circle around the North Star. In the winter, the handle of the dipper will be pointing down (Fig. 6-2). In the spring, the dipper will be upside down (Fig. 6-3). In the summer, the handle will be pointing up (Fig. 6-4). In the autumn, the dipper will be rightside up (Fig. 6-5).

Notice the two bright stars in the front of the dipper. These are the two stars farthest from the handle. They point to the North Star and are called the pointer stars. Estimate the distance between these two stars. Count about five of these spaces on a line from the end of the Big Dipper, and you should find the North Star. The North Star is also the end star in the handle of the Little Dipper.

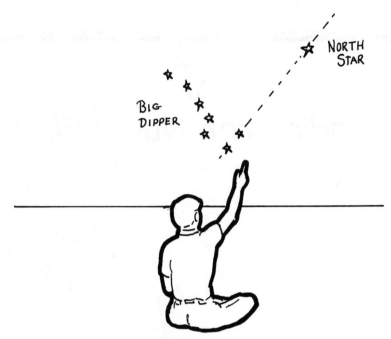

Fig. 6-1. *To find the North Star, face the northern half of the sky and look for the Big Dipper.*

Fig. 6-2. *In winter, the handle of the Big Dipper will be pointing down.*

Fig. 6-3. In the spring, the Big Dipper will be upside down.

Fig. 6-4. In the summer, the handle of the Big Dipper will be pointing up.

Fig. 6-5. *In the autumn, the Big Dipper will be rightside up.*

7

Finding Your Latitude from the North Star

Materials
- 1 PIECE OF POSTER BOARD (ABOUT 5×5 INCHES)
- PLASTIC DRINKING STRAW
- STRING (ABOUT 8 INCHES LONG)
- PAPER CLIP
- SMALL WEIGHT

Materials
(SINKER, WASHER, ETC.)
- SCOTCH TAPE
- PROTRACTOR
- PENCIL
- SCISSORS

Draw a line on two sides of the posterboard ½ inch from the edge (Fig. 7-1). Place the protractor as shown in Fig. 7-2 and mark the angles, from 0 to 90 degrees, on the posterboard. Mark off and label the degrees in units of 10; 0, 10, 20, 30 etc. Make a smaller mark halfway between to represent each 5 degrees; 5, 15, 25 etc. Trim off the excess part of the card (Fig. 7-3). Punch a small hole where the lines meet and thread one end of the string through this hole. Tie the end of the string to the paper clip to keep the string from slipping back through. Tie the weight to the other end of the string. Next, tape the straw to the top edge of the card—the edge closest to where the lines meet and the 90 degree mark. When you sight the North Star through the straw, the string will mark the degree of latitude of your location (Fig. 7-4).

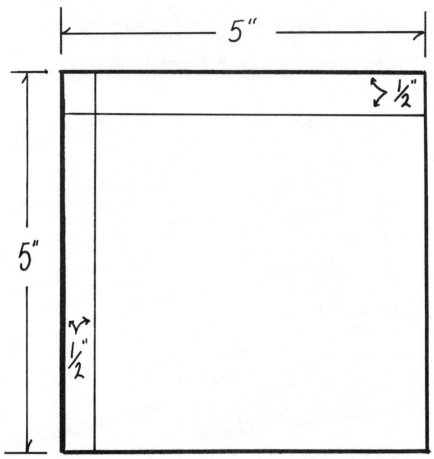

Fig. 7-1. *Draw lines 1/2 inch from the edge of the posterboard.*

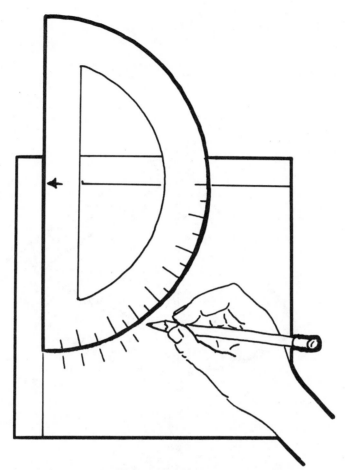

Fig. 7-2. *Mark the angles from 0 to 90 degrees.*

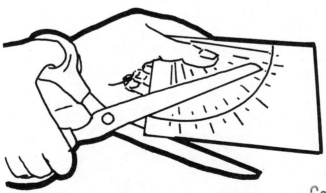

Fig. 7-3. *Cut the excess material from the card.*

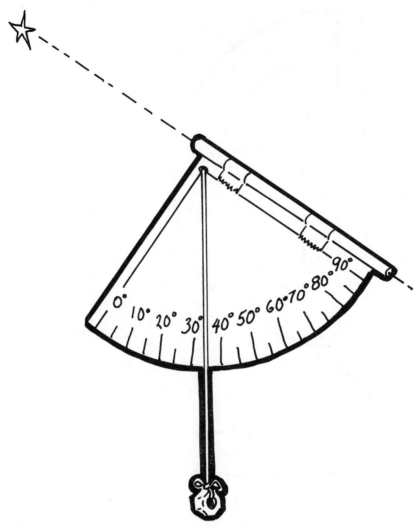

Fig. 7-4. *Sight through the straw at the North Star to find your degree of latitude.*

8
Shadows on a Map

Materials
- RELIEF MAP (SHOWING LANDSCAPE)
- FLASHLIGHT
- SHEET OF PAPER

Because most maps are flat, there had to be some way of showing the steepness of mountains. Map makers use a series of lines drawn close together to create the effect of shadows.

Make several folds in the paper something like an accordion (Fig. 8-1). Unfold the paper, and place it flat on a table. Position the flashlight above the upper corner of the paper (Fig. 8-2). Let the light shine across the paper.

Shadows will appear on one side of the folds (Fig. 8-3). The shadows are wide and show a shallow slope. Push the paper together from the ends. Notice how the shadows show steepness (Fig. 8-4). You can see how the shadows on a flat map show the slope of mountains.

Fig. 8-1. Fold the paper into sections.

Fig. 8-2. Place the flashlight near an upper corner.

Fig. 8-3. The light will cast shadows on the folds.

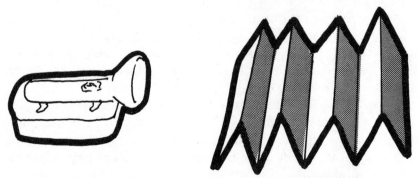

Fig. 8-4. Push the paper together to create steeper shadows.

9
Mountains and Contour Lines

Materials
- TOPOGRAPHIC MAP (ONE THAT SHOWS CONTOUR LINES)
- MODELING CLAY
- BOWL
- DEEP PAN OR LARGE POT
- TOOTHPICK
- RULER

Materials
- WATER

Examine the map and you will notice a pattern of lines. These are contour lines. A contour line connects all points of the same elevation at a particular area.

Turn the bowl upside down and place it on a flat surface. Apply the modeling clay to the outside of the bowl (Fig. 9-1). Shape the clay in the form of a small mountain. The bowl is just to be a base for the mountain. Cover the bowl completely (Fig. 9-2). Place the mountain into the pot. Stand the ruler next to the mountain and pour in one inch of water (Fig. 9-3). Use the toothpick to draw a line around the mountain at the edge of the water (Fig. 9-4). This is a contour line. Pour in another inch of water. Mark another line around the mountain. Continue adding the same amount of water, and marking lines until you reach the top of the mountain. Remove the mountain from the water and place it on a flat surface. Look down at the mountain from directly over its center (Fig. 9-5). You will see how contour lines show the shape of a mountain. Where the lines are close together, the slope is steeper. The numbers in the lines represent the elevation of the lines. In Fig. 9-6, the space between contours is 10, with the elevation at 650. The units can represent feet or meters, depending on the map.

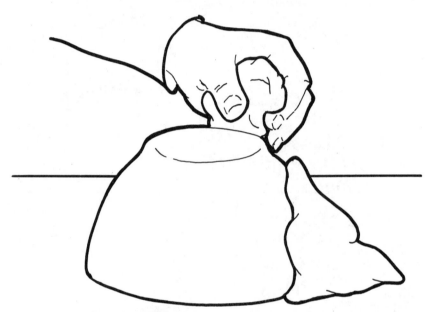

Fig. 9-1. *Apply clay to the outside of the bowl.*

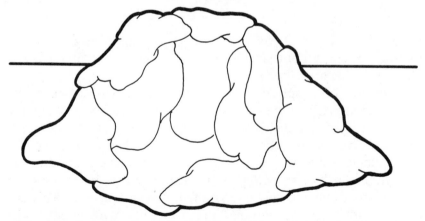

Fig. 9-2. *Cover the bowl completely and shape it into the form of a mountain.*

Fig. 9-3. *Use the ruler to measure 1 inch of water.*

Fig. 9-4. *Use the toothpick to mark the water line.*

Fig. 9-5. *Contour lines show the shape of the mountain.*

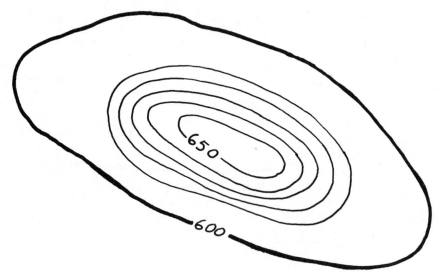

Fig. 9-6. *The elevation of this mountain is 650.*

10
Depression Contours

Materials

BOWL
PENCIL
RULER
WATER

Stand the ruler in the bowl and pour in one inch of water. Use the pencil to mark the edge of the water line. This is a contour line. Add another inch of water and mark another line. Continue adding water and marking lines until the bowl is full. Empty the water and look straight down at the lines. You can see contour lines that show the shape of the bowl (Fig. 10-1). Imagine the bowl is sunk in the ground, but on a map this would look just like a hill. To avoid confusion, map makers show depressions with depression contours (Fig. 10-2). These depression contours have short lines on one side of the contour lines. These short lines point downslope. You can mark small lines inside the bowl to show that it is a depression. In the illustration, the contour interval is 10. The top of the hole is at 600, whereas the bottom elevation is 570 (Fig. 10-3).

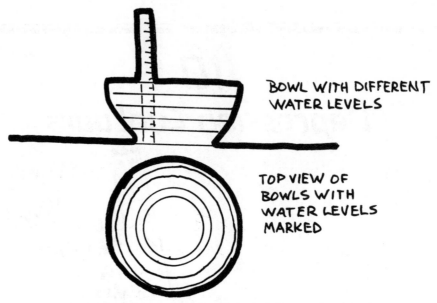

BOWL WITH DIFFERENT
WATER LEVELS

TOP VIEW OF
BOWLS WITH
WATER LEVELS
MARKED

Fig. 10-1. *Contour lines show the shape of the inside of the bowl.*

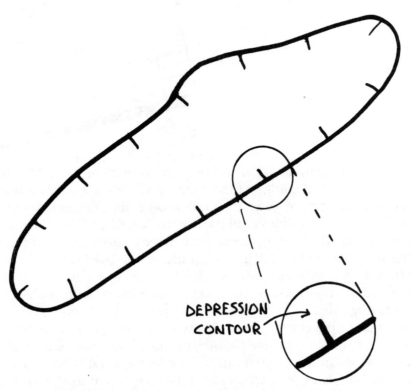

DEPRESSION
CONTOUR

Fig. 10-2. *Illustration of a depression contour line.*

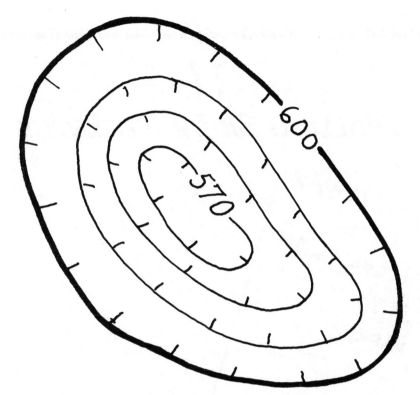

Fig. 10-3. *The bottom of this hole has an elevation of 570.*

11
Plotting Slope Patterns

Look at the map and find the contour line that represents a hill. Place the sheet of paper across the center of the hill. Use the ruler to measure units of 10 straight up on the paper, and on line with each contour line. These units represent elevation. The first contour line represents the bottom of the hill, so begin measuring from the second line. Make a small dot at each elevation (Fig. 11-1). Connect the dots and you will have a rough pattern of the slope of the hill (Fig. 11-2).

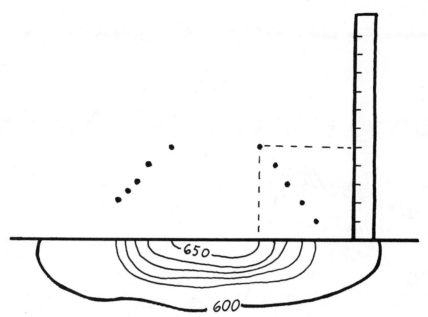

Fig. 11-1. *Use a ruler to make the dots for each elevation.*

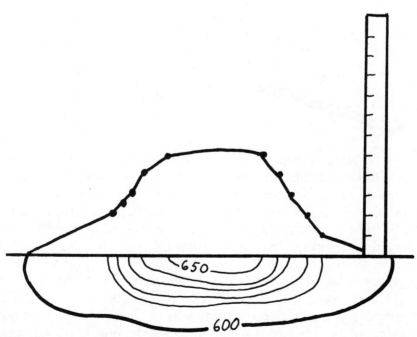

Fig. 11-2. *Connect the dots to show a rough pattern of the slope of the hill.*

12

Reading Distance on a Road Map

Look at the road map and locate the legend, or key, that displays
the symbols that are used on the map (Fig. 12-1). Notice one of the
symbols represent miles between points. You can see a large
number between two stars. This is the total mileage between cities
or junctions that are marked by a star. In Fig. 12-2, it is 60 miles
from the star on the left to the crossroad, and 30 miles from the
crossroad to the next star. Look at the road map and select a
highway between two cities. You might find something similar to
Fig. 12-3. Notice the highway between Smith City and Bitter
Springs. The numbers on the left side of the road represent the
number of miles between the towns along the highway. Starting at
Smith City; 17 miles to The Gap, 8 miles to Cedar Ridge, and 18

miles to Bitter Springs. The larger number on the right side of the highway represents the miles between Smith City and Bitter Springs—the cities marked by the stars. Map makers have provided an easy way to find the mileage without doing any measuring.

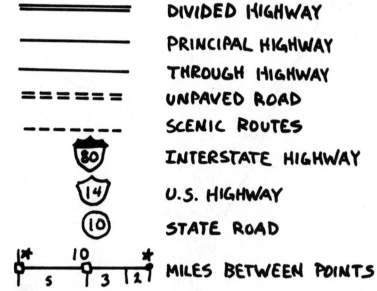

Fig. 12-1. *The legend identifies the symbols that are used on the map.*

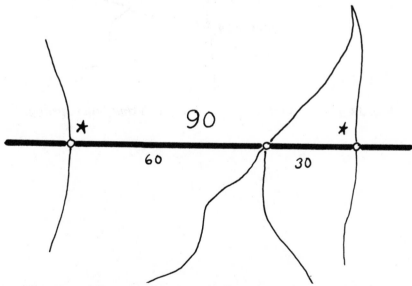

Fig. 12-2. *The larger numbers between the two stars represents the total mileage between the two stars.*

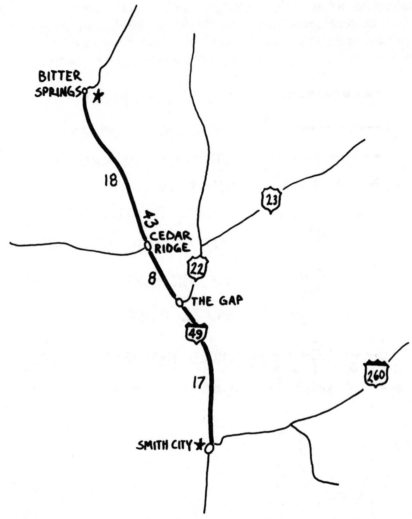

Fig. 12-3. *It is 43 miles between Smith City and Bitter Springs.*

13

Measuring Distance

Look at the map and find the legend. There should be a line, or lines, representing the scale of miles. It should look something like Fig. 13-1. (The illustrations in this book are for examples only and are not to scale.) Notice the number of miles that are covered in one inch. You have some idea of distance just by estimating the number of inches. To be more accurate, spread the map on a flat surface and place the end of the ruler at the point you want to measure from (Fig. 13-2). Roads seldom run straight for long so you will have to turn the ruler to follow the road (Fig. 13-3). Measure as accurately as you can to the other point. When you know the total number of inches between the two points, multiply by the number of miles per inch to get the distance.

If you don't have a ruler, use the straight edge of a piece of paper. Make a mark at the starting point, turn the paper to follow the road, and make a mark at the destination (Fig. 13-4). If one edge of the paper is not long enough, use the other side. Place the edge of the paper next to the scale of miles on the map, and calculate the distance.

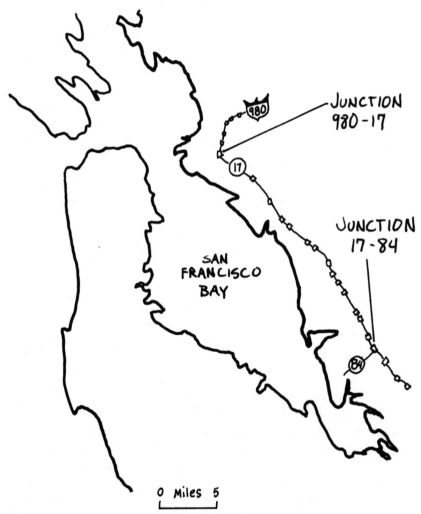

Fig. 13-1. *The map has a line that represents the scale of miles.*

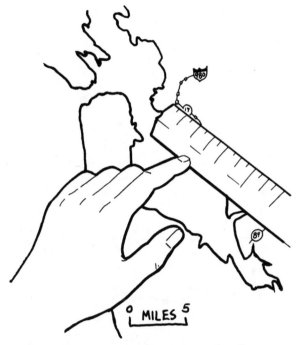

Fig. 13-2. *Use a ruler to measure the distance.*

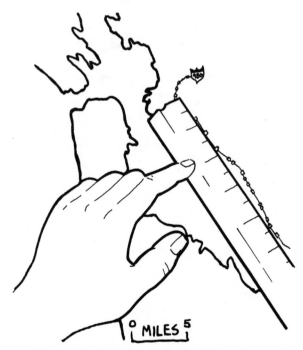

Fig. 13-3. *Turn the ruler to follow the road.*

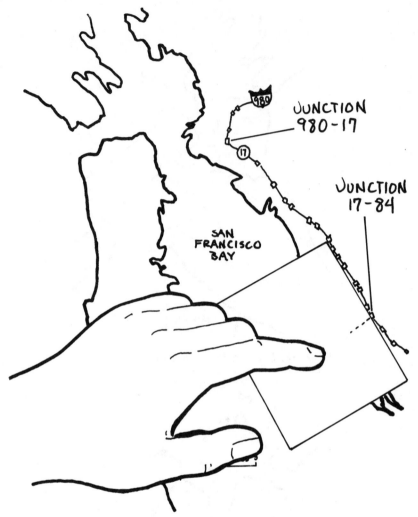

Fig. 13-4. *The straight edge of a piece of paper can be used to measure the distance.*

14
Calculating Range

Imagine a typical car that has a 15-gallon fuel tank. You don't want to run it dry, so you might choose 12 gallons as usable fuel for traveling. If the car gets about 20 miles for each gallon of fuel used, you can see you have a range of about 240 miles. Place the map on a flat surface. Tie a knot in one end of the string. Find the scale of miles on the map and place the knot at the 0 mark. Stretch the string along the scale of miles and measure 240 miles. Tie another knot at this point (Fig. 14-1). Hold the first knot on your location. Stretch the string out across the map to find the range of your car (Fig. 14-2). Remember that you can't usually drive from one place to another in a straight line so you have to reduce the range to compensate. This method will give you a reasonably accurate range for an aircraft.

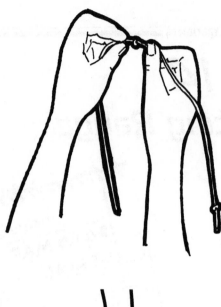

Fig. 14-1. *Tie a knot in the string to represent the range.*

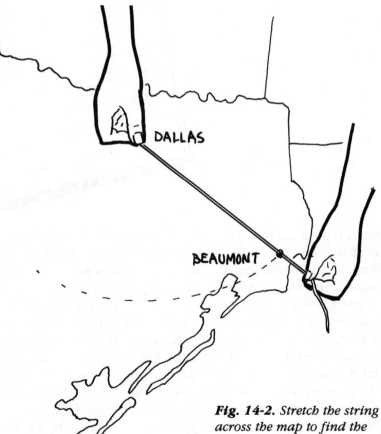

DALLAS

BEAUMONT

Fig. 14-2. *Stretch the string across the map to find the range.*

15
Orientating a Map

Spread the map on a flat surface, and imagine it as a flat, shrunken model of the landscape. Find your location on the map. Assume you wanted to go from your house to a place you had never been to before, a city park, for example. You find the park on the map, and you see the direction from your house. Plot the route on the map (Fig. 15-1). You might have to turn right on one street, or left on another. Transfer the directions from the map to the landscape. Line up the streets on the map with the streets where you live (Fig. 15-2). You are orientating the map with the landscape. You might have to read the map upside down, or sideways. If you need to go right on the map to get to the park, it will be right on the landscape. Most maps have the top of the map pointing north.

Fig. 15-1. Mark the route to the park on the map.

Fig. 15-2. Line up the map with the streets.

16
Making a Compass

Materials
- MAGNET
- STEEL NEEDLE
- FINE THREAD (ABOUT 8 INCHES LONG)
- WOODEN PENCIL
- DRINKING GLASS
- SMALL PIECE OF PAPER (ABOUT 1 X 2 INCHES)

Fold the paper in half to make a 1-inch square. Thread the needle and tie a knot at the end of the thread. The knot is to keep the thread from pulling through the paper. Open the folded paper a little and push the needle through the center from the inside of the fold (Fig. 16-1). Carefully pull the needle through the paper stopping when the knot reaches the paper. Remove the thread from the needle and tie the free end of the thread around the middle of the pencil. The length of thread should suspend the needle approximately an inch above the bottom of the glass. Magnetize the needle by stroking it about 20 times with one end of the magnet. With the paper spread tentlike, insert the needle horizontally through both sides of the paper (Fig. 16-2). Center the needle so that it will balance. Lower the needle into the glass so that it is free to turn. The needle will swing a few times, and then it will align itself north and south (Fig. 16-3).

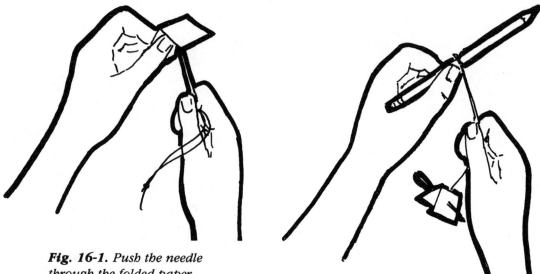

Fig. 16-1. *Push the needle through the folded paper.*

Fig. 16-2. *Tie the thread to the pencil.*

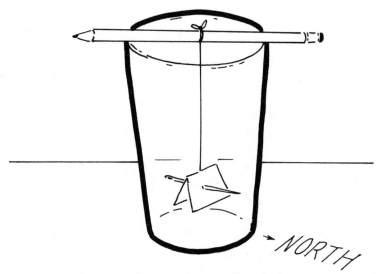

Fig. 17-3. *One end of the needle will point north.*

17
Magnetic Deviation

Place the compass on a flat surface and allow the needle to settle in one direction (Fig. 17-1). Slowly bring the head of the hammer near the needle. Watch the needle change directions (Fig. 17-2). Iron or steel objects brought near a magnetic compass will cause the needle to give false readings.

Fig. 17-1. *Place the compass on a flat surface.*

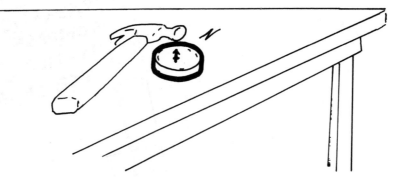

Fig. 17-2. *Magnetic deviation is the deflection of a compass needle due to outside influences such as iron or steel.*

18
North and Magnetic North

Examine the area of the earth near the top of the map. You can see that the North Pole is at the top where all the lines of longitude come together. However, the magnetic North Pole is further south, near Prince Of Wales Island in Canada (Fig. 18-1). It is roughly at 75 degrees north latitude, and 100 degrees west longitude. Because the magnetic axis of the earth is not the same as the true north and south axis, magnetic compasses rarely point true north. The angle between the true North Pole and the magnetic North Pole is called the *angle of magnetic declination*, or *variation* (Fig. 18-2). The magnetic North Pole tends to drift somewhat, causing these angles to change. Charts that show magnetic declination angles must be upgraded every few years.

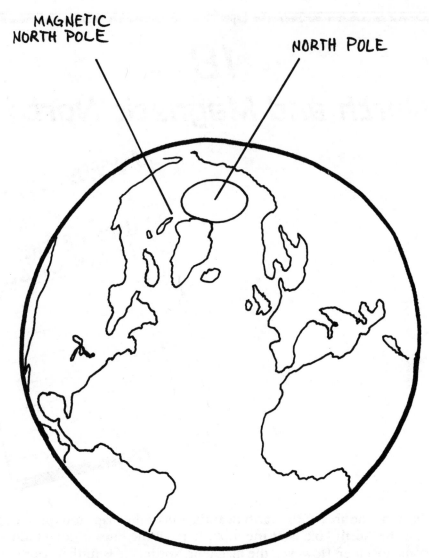

Fig. 18-1. *Magnetic North Pole is south of the true North Pole.*

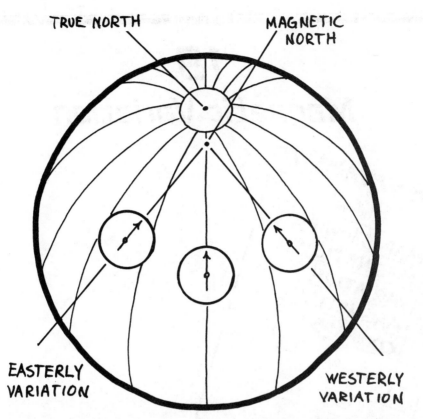

Fig. 18-2. *Magnetic variation is the angler difference between the magnetic north and true north.*

19
Magnetic Variation

Materials

- MAP SHOWING MAGNETIC VARIATION
- MAGNETIC COMPASS

Examine the map and find a location near one of the lines that show the magnetic variation. If the location is near the Mississippi River, the magnetic variation is 0 degrees (Fig. 19-1). The compass is pointing about true north. But if the location is near San Diego, the magnetic variation is about 15 degrees east (Fig. 19-2). Near Maine, it is about 20 degrees west (Fig. 19-3). To get a true heading, this angle is added to the compass heading. To convert a true heading into a compass heading, subtract the variation. For example, if you were in San Diego with a compass, and you wanted to go due east, or 90 degrees, you would go on a magnetic heading of 75 degrees. When you subtract 15 degrees (the easterly variation) from the true heading, 90 degrees, you get 75 degrees, the compass heading (Fig. 19-4).

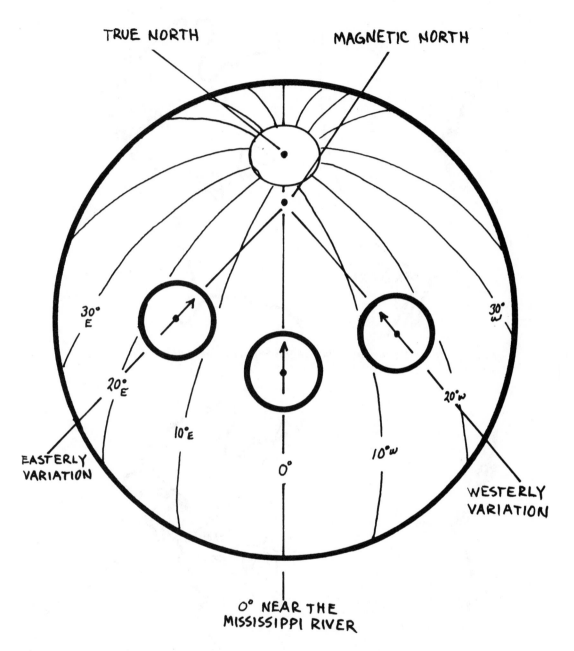

Fig. 19-1. *Near the Mississippi River a magnetic compass points about true north.*

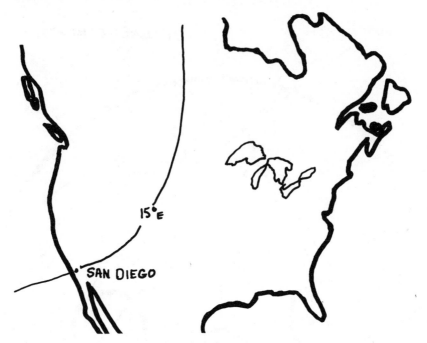

Fig. 19-2. *Near San Diego the magnetic variation is about 15 degrees east.*

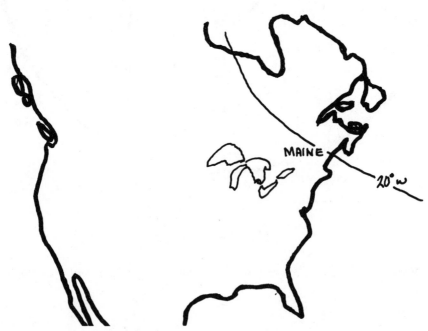

Fig. 19-3. *Near Maine the magnetic variation is about 20 degrees west.*

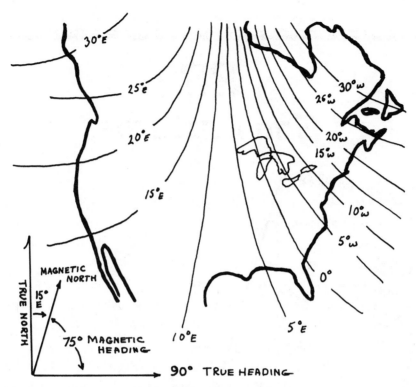

Fig. 19-4. *To convert a true heading into a magnetic heading subtract easterly variation and add westerly variation.*

20

Grid Patterns

Materials

RULER
PENCIL
PAPER

Imagine a 25-acre pasture that contains horses. Draw a square to represent the pasture and make a dot to represent each horse (Fig. 20-1). You might want to use a scale in which 1 square inch represents 1 acre. You might have 100 horses—100 horses for 25 acres. You notice that some areas have more horses, others have fewer. To show which areas have the most horses, draw a grid made of 1-acre squares, and count the horses in each square (Fig. 20-2). This will express the densities of horses per acre (Fig. 20-3).

A simpler way to show density is to make a legend and use shading patterns to represent numbers (Fig. 20-4). Replace the numbers on the map with a shaded pattern that corresponds to that number. This shows at a glance the relationship between areas and quantities. Dot maps are more accurate, but by using a legend to show different categories, we've lost some accuracy in exchange for conveniency.

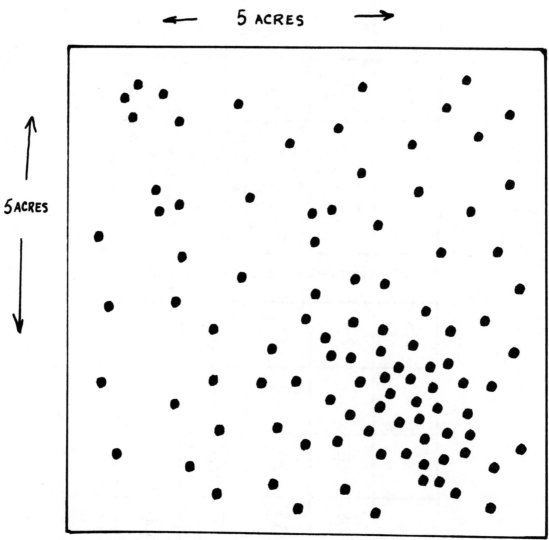

Fig. 20-1. Make a dot to represent each horse in the pasture.

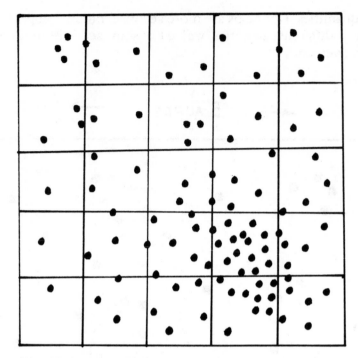

Fig. 20-2. *Count the horses in each square in the grid.*

4	2	2	3	3
3	2	3	3	2
1	4	2	6	4
1	3	8	15	5
1	2	5	10	6

Fig. 20-3. *The grid represents the densities of horses per acre.*

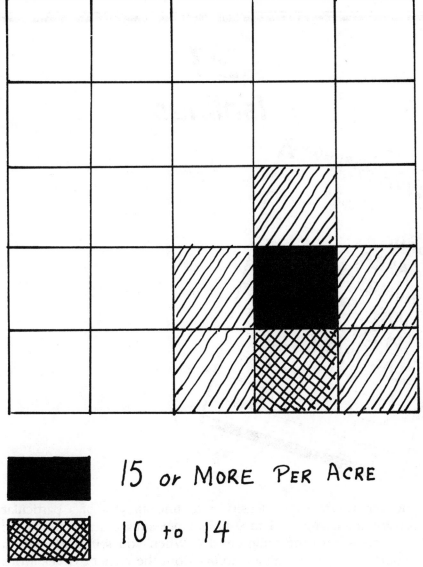

	15 or MORE PER ACRE
	10 to 14
	5 to 9
	UNDER 5 PER ACRE

Fig. 20-4. *Shaded patterns can represent numbers of different densities.*

21
Isolines

Another way to show density is to find an area of a particular density, for example, 5 to 9 horses per square acre. Notice the other areas with the same density. When you join areas with a smooth line, you create an *isoline* from the ancient Greek word *iso*, meaning equal (Fig. 21-1). Find other areas of another density (10−14) and connect that area by a line. Connect the area with a density of 15 or more horses, and let the remaining area represent the under-5 density (Fig. 21-2). You have created an isoline map. This still might be confusing to read. Use a color or shaded pattern for each category (Fig. 21-3). Dark colors, or shades, tend to represent more density, whereas lighter shades represent less density. With the shaded areas, it should be easier to see the pattern of densities for a particular area.

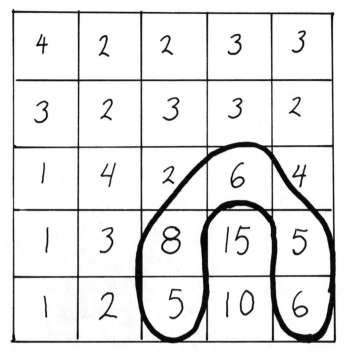

Fig. 21-1. *An isoline represents areas with the same density.*

4	2	2	3	3
3	2	3	3	2
1	4	2	6	4
1	3	8	15	5
1	2	5	10	6

Fig. 21-2. *The unshaded area represents a density of 5 or less.*

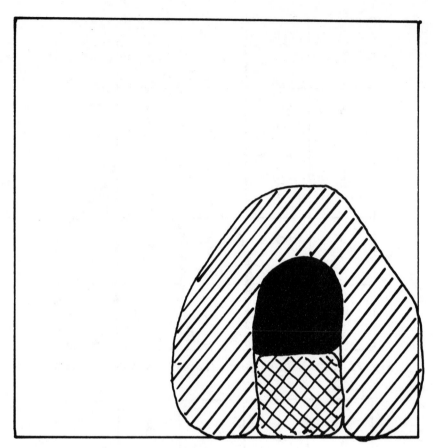

Fig. 21-3. *Shaded patterns represent areas of similar densities.*

22
Political Regions

Examine the map of North America shown in Fig. 22-1. You can see only a continent. Figure 22-2 shows the dotted lines of the boundaries between Canada, the United States, and Mexico. Place the paper over the map and trace the outline of North America. Include the dotted lines for the boundaries. Dotted lines help, but the map can be made easier to read. Shade, or color, the area inside each boundary. By using different colors, or shading, the different political regions become clearer (Fig. 22-3).

Maps that show the political regions are common. They provide a useful guide to help us see and understand the unfamiliar world that we live in.

Fig. 22-1. *Map of North America.*

Fig. 22-2. *Dotted lines representing boundaries.*

Fig. 22-3. *Shaded patterns represent different political regions.*

23
Middle, Average, Median, and Mean

Materials

- WORLD MAP OR GLOBE
- CITY MAP
- TRACING PAPER
- PENCIL
- RULER

Examine the map of the world, and notice the different surface area. The earth has a surface area of about 197 million square miles—that alone would be a lot to study. Geographers are interested in what takes place above the surface, as well as below. They also study people and what they do. To describe any of the information in a simple form, geographers let one thing represent many things. They use terms such as average, mean, middle, and median. Imagine four students who are taking a test. Three are not familiar with the subject, but one is. One student receives a grade of 30, two receive grades of 35, and one receives 100. To find the average, add the total scores and divide by the number of students (4). You find an average grade of 50. This is not a fair representation of the students, because one student brought the average well above the rest of the students. With few numbers, you receive unpredictable results. Use the largest population as possible to find the average.

Examine the map of the city (Fig. 23-1). Draw a grid like the one in Fig. 23-2, and place it over the map. Notice the number of buildings inside each square. You can see that some areas have little or no buildings, whereas others have more (Fig. 23-3). Count the number of buildings in each square (Fig. 23-4). Add the numbers together to find the total number of buildings that are inside the grid. Assume that you counted 150. Divide the total by the number of squares in the grid (150 divided by 25). This is the density of a single representative square that reflects a larger number of squares. Here, there are an average of 6 buildings for each square mile.

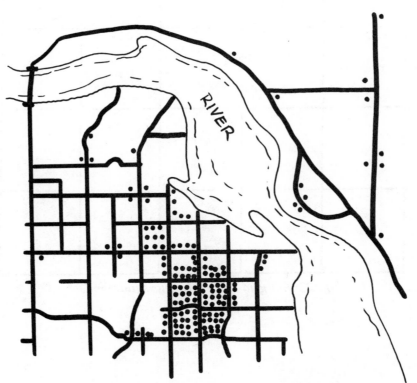

Fig. 23-1. *A city map that shows buildings.*

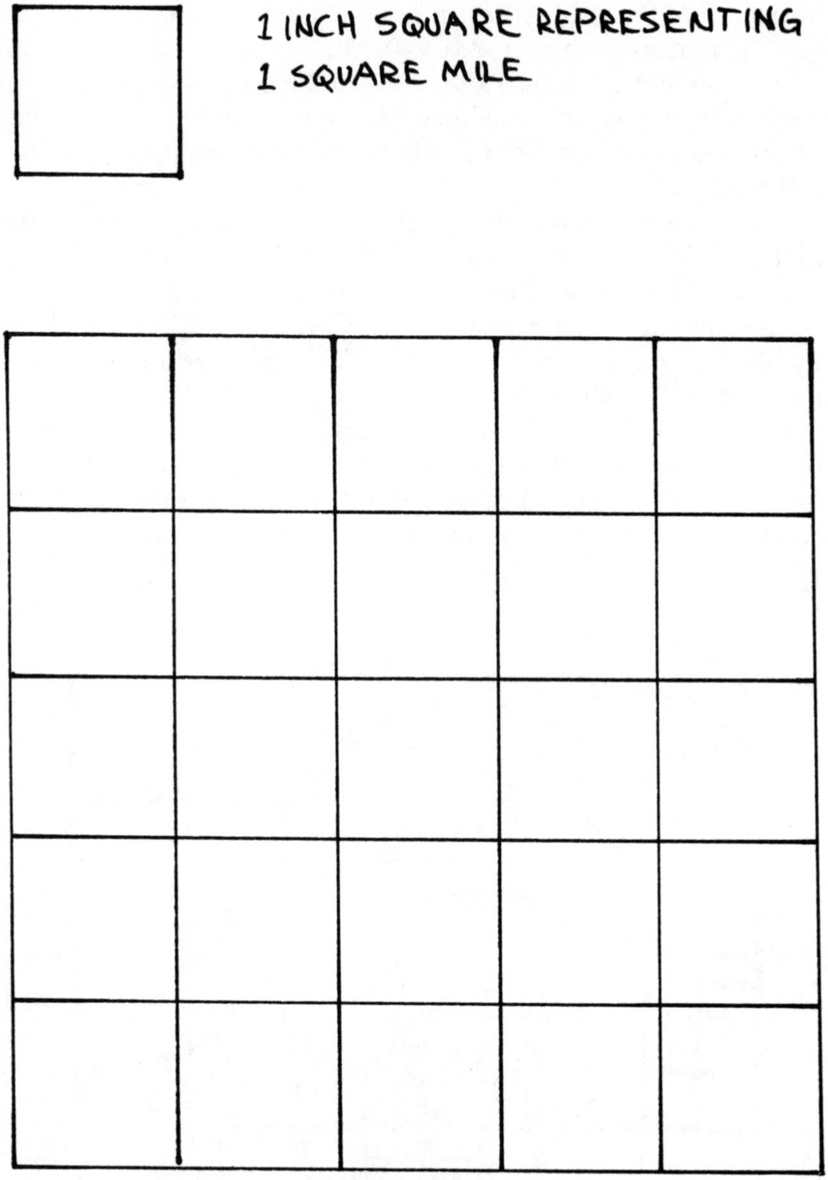

1 INCH SQUARE REPRESENTING
1 SQUARE MILE

Fig. 23-2. *A grid that represents square miles.*

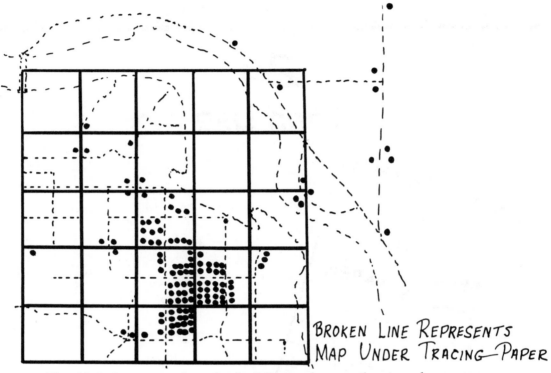

Fig. 23-3. *Some areas have few buildings, whereas other areas have many.*

BROKEN LINE REPRESENTS
MAP UNDER TRACING PAPER

Fig. 23-4. *Figures representing the number of buildings in each square mile.*

0	1	0	0	1
1	3	1	0	1
0	3	18	0	2
1	1	25	29	3
0	2	20	0	0

Middle, Average, Median, and Mean **73**

24
Land Use

Study the map, and notice how the land is being used. Place the paper over the map, and outline different areas. Label each area by the way it is used (Fig. 24-1). You might find a water reservoir. It also can be a lake that is surrounded by a park and recreation area. Locate the schools. They should be in an area of homes and low traffic. The civic center and business should be in a commercial area that can handle a high flow of traffic. If you live near the ocean, you might find an area set aside for loading and unloading ships (Fig. 24-2). This area will probably have warehouses to store the material until it is transported to other destinations locally (Fig. 24-3).

As our population grows, it not only is important to describe our landscape, but what takes place on it. The future use of the landscape is an important part of geography. The highways we use cost millions of dollars. Where will new ones be built? Where should the next multimillion-dollar school be built? Geographers and engineers look for patterns—patterns of population and traffic flow, for example. By studying as much data as possible, they can decide the best use for the land that is available.

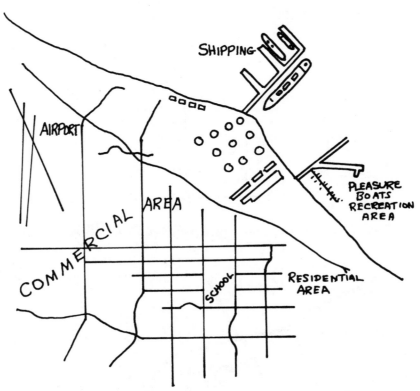

Fig. 24-1. City map showing how the land is used.

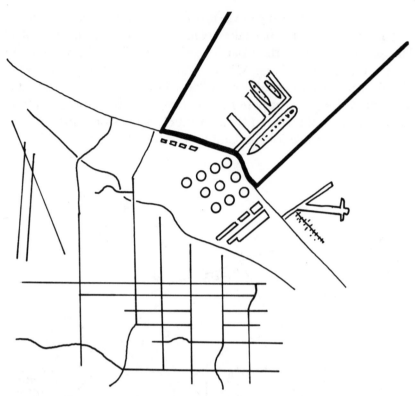

Fig. 24-2. *City map showing areas set aside for docking ships.*

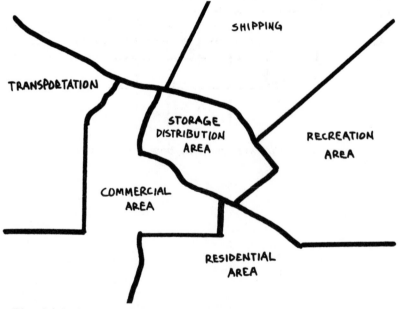

SHIPPING

TRANSPORTATION

STORAGE
DISTRIBUTION
AREA

RECREATION
AREA

COMMERCIAL
AREA

RESIDENTIAL
AREA

Fig. 24-3. *Storage and distribution areas are located near docks.*

25
Neighborhood Research

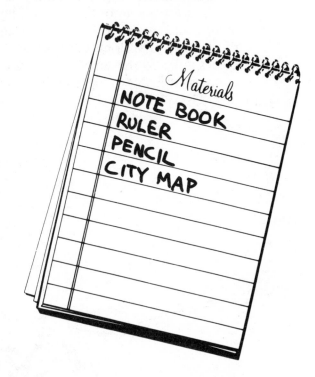

Locate your neighborhood on the map. Find the streets near your house. Notice the traffic on these streets. One street probably has more traffic than the others. It carries a large flow of traffic that comes from the side streets of residential areas, much like small streams feeding a river. You can see how stop signs and traffic lights help maintain a smooth, orderly flow of traffic. You also can see that at certain times of day, the traffic is much greater than at other times. You can plot this information on a graph. Take a notebook, a pencil, and a watch to a place near the busiest street (Fig. 25-1). Count the number of cars that pass in 5 minutes at 3:00 PM, 4:00 PM, 5:00 PM, 6:00 PM, and 7:00 PM. At 3:00, you might count 20 cars. At 4:00, you might count 35 cars. At 5:00, you might count 60 cars. At 6:00, you might see 30 cars, and at 7:00, you might be back down to 20 cars.

To make a bar graph, draw a grid 4 × 6 inches, and mark off the time of day along the left edge. Mark the rate of the flow of traffic along the bottom. Plot the traffic for each time of day (Fig. 25-2). You can see that the traffic increases from 3:00 and peaks at 5:00, then decreases. This tells you that the traffic is largely made up of commuters who are coming home from work.

To plot this information on a line graph, draw a grid 3 × 5 inches, and mark off the flow of traffic along the left edge. Mark the time of day along the bottom. Make a dot on the grid that corresponds to the time and the flow of traffic. Draw a line that connects the dots to represent the traffic at a particular time of day (Fig. 25-3). This also shows that the traffic peaks at 5:00 PM.

Fig. 25-1. *Record the traffic on a busy street.*

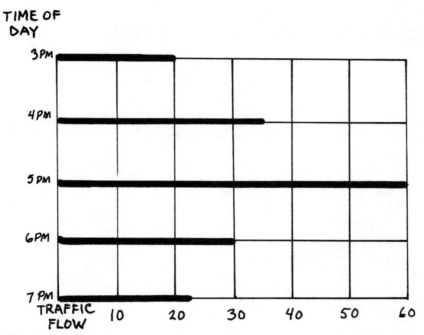

Fig. 25-2. *A bar graph showing the flow of traffic and the time of day.*

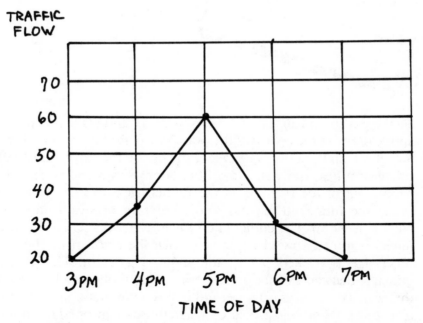

Fig. 25-3. *A line graph showing the flow of traffic and the time of day.*

26

The Earth's Crust and Volcanoes

Materials

- METAL POT
- SMALL METAL FUNNEL
- WATER
- STOVE

Fill the pot about half full of water (Fig. 26-1), and place the funnel upside down in the center of the pot. Only part of the spout of the funnel should be above water. Place the pot on the stove (Fig. 26-2) and slowly heat the water to a boil. Soon, steam and water will bubble out of the opening in the funnel. Heat causes the water inside the funnel to expand into a mixture of steam and hot bubbles of water. The cooler and heavier water that is outside the funnel is forced down by gravity to take the place of the heated water that is pushed out of the spout (Fig. 26-3). This is the principle that causes volcanoes to erupt. Hot, molten rock beneath the earth's crust gives off gases and builds up tremendous pressure (Fig. 26-4). When this pressure breaks through an opening in the earth, the volcano erupts (Fig. 26-5).

Fig. 26-1. *Fill the pot with water.*

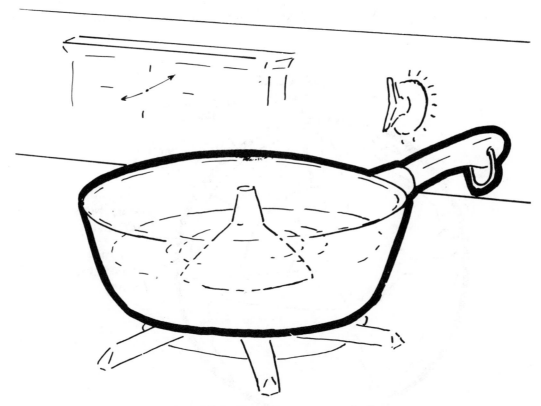

Fig. 26-2. *Heat the water to a boil.*

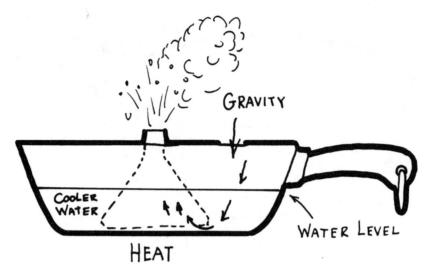

Fig. 26-3. *Steam and water will bubble out the opening in the funnel.*

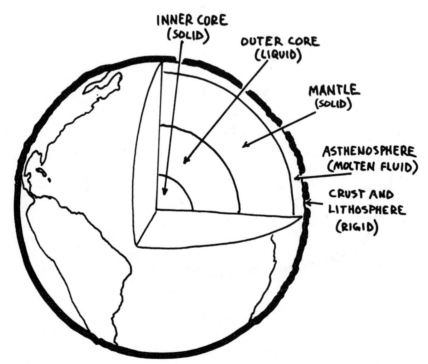

Fig. 26-4. *Molten rock beneath the earth's crust is under pressure.*

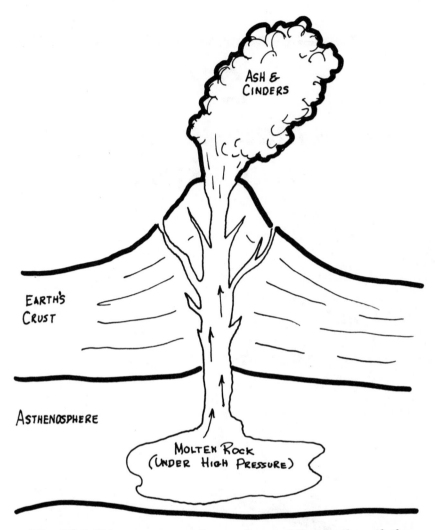

Fig. 26-5. *Volcanoes erupt when molten rock breaks through the earth's crust.*

27
How Mountains Form and Earthquakes Happen

Roll each color clay into a thick sheet. Place the two sheets of paper on a smooth, flat surface (Fig. 27-1). Allow the edge of one piece of paper to overlap the other about an inch. Stack the sheets of clay on both pieces of paper to form three layers of different colors (Fig. 27-2). These layers represent different layers of rock formations. The two sheets of paper represent the fluid layer of molten rock that is beneath the earth's crust. Push each end of the clay toward the middle (Fig. 27-3). The layers will rise in places and begin to fold. This can represent the formation of a mountain range caused by extreme pressure from below (Fig. 27-4). Mountains are also formed by erosion. If you continue to push from the sides, the layers can tear and form faults like we have in the earth's crust (Fig. 27-5). Push the clay forward on one side of the fault and back on the other side. When the earth's crust suddenly slips along a fault, it is an earthquake. California's San Andreas fault is well known for its earthquakes (Fig. 27-6).

Fig. 27-1. *Place the papers on a flat surface.*

Fig. 27-2. *Stack the layers of clay on the papers.*

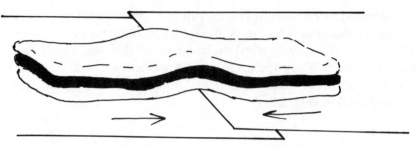

Fig. 27-3. Push the ends of the clay toward the middle.

FORMING A HILL

Fig. 27-4. Mountain ranges are formed by extreme pressure from below.

FORMING A FAULT

Fig. 27-5. Continued pressure can form faults in the earth's crust.

Fig. 27-6. *The San Andreas fault in California.*

28
Midocean Ridges

Examine the map and find the midocean ridges (Fig. 28-1). These are large, underwater volcanic mountain ranges found in all the oceans. They are called midocean ridges even though they are not always in the exact middle of the ocean. The best known and most studied is the Mid-Atlantic Ridge (Fig. 28-2). It runs the entire length of the ocean and is from 300 to 1200 miles wide. Ridges are formed when hot, molten rock pushes up through the earth's crust (Fig. 28-3). A *trough*, or *rift*, is often found in the crest of these midocean ridges. The rift is a big crack in the ridge. The rift in the Mid-Atlantic Ridge is, in places, 30 miles wide and twice as deep as the Grand Canyon. Earthquakes and volcanic activity are common along midocean ridges. When eruptions occur, the molten rock flows down the slopes of the ridge and cools, forming new material. In some places along the midocean ridges, the volcanic activity was great enough to form huge masses of lava that protruded above the water and created an island. Iceland is one of these islands (Fig. 28-4). As the molten rock oozes up through cracks in the midocean ridges (Fig. 28-5), the new material pushes on rigid, sometimes 80 miles thick, plates that make up the earth's surface. This causes the ocean floor to spread and moves the continents farther apart (Fig. 28-6).

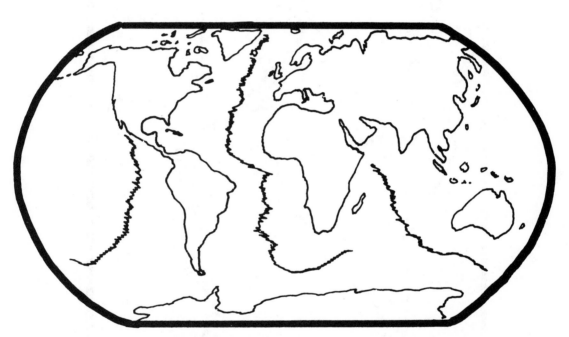

Fig. 28-1. *Midocean ridges are found in all the oceans.*

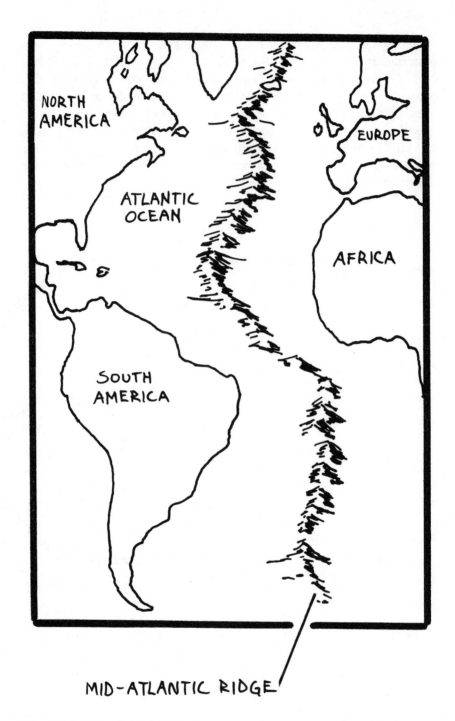

Fig. 28-2. *The Mid-Atlantic Ridge runs the entire length of the Atlantic Ocean.*

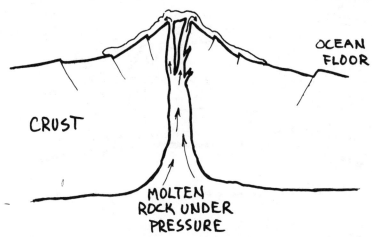

Fig. 28-3. *Underwater ridges are formed when molten rock pushes up through the earth's crust.*

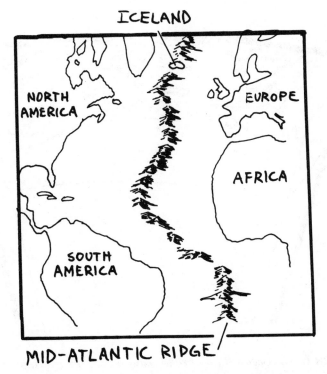

Fig. 28-4. *Iceland is an island created by volcanic activity.*

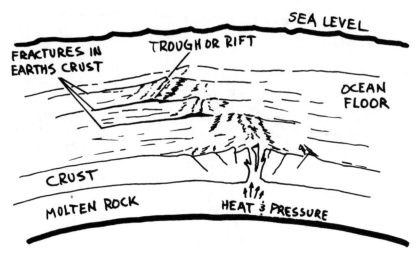

Fig. 28-5. *Molten rock oozes up through cracks in the ocean floor.*

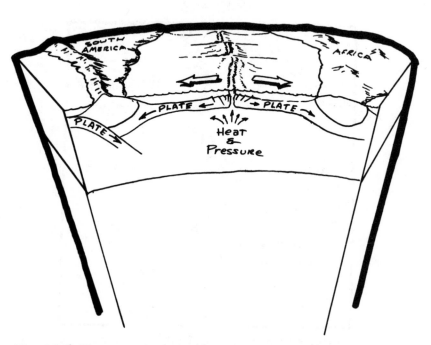

Fig. 28-6. *The ocean floor spreads and moves the continents further apart.*

29
Land Mass and Continental Drift

Materials
- WORLD MAP OR GLOBE
- TRACING PAPER
- PENCIL
- SCISSORS

Place the tracing paper over the map, and trace the outline of each continent on the paper (Fig. 29-1). Use the scissors to cut the pattern of each continent from the paper (Fig. 29-2). Put the patterns on a flat surface and fit them together like a puzzle (Fig. 29-3). You will see that the east side of South America almost matches the west side of Africa. About 150 million years ago, the continents probably looked like Fig. 29-4. The plates that carry the continents drifted away from each other as a lower layer of rock filled in the area between the plates. By 60 million years ago, the Atlantic Ocean had created a great expanse between North America and Europe, which looked like Fig. 29-5. The plates continued to drift at a rate of about an inch a year, until the continents reached their present positions, about 3000 miles apart. The plates are still moving. New rock formations build on one edge of the plates, pushing the plates apart. Because the earth is not getting any larger, the old edge slips beneath the crust to be recycled for the future (Fig. 29-6). Fifty million years in the future the map of the continents might be similar to Fig. 29-7.

Fig. 29-1. *Outline each continent on the tracing paper.*

Fig. 29-2. *Use scissors to cut out the continents.*

Fig. 29-3. *Fit the continents together like a puzzle.*

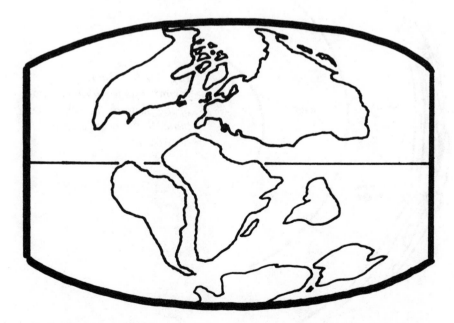

Fig. 29-4. *The probable location of the continents about 150 million years ago.*

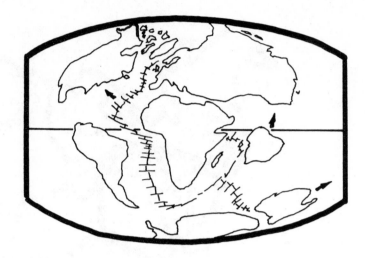

Fig. 29-5. *About 60 million years ago a great expanse existed between North America and Europe.*

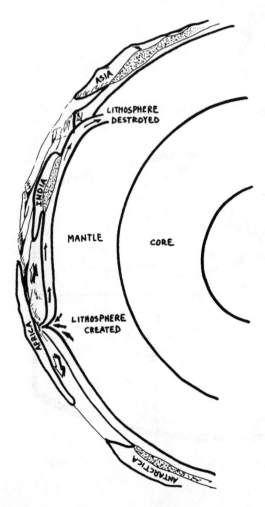

Fig. 29-6. *New rock formations form on one edge of the plate as the old edge slips beneath the crust and is destroyed.*

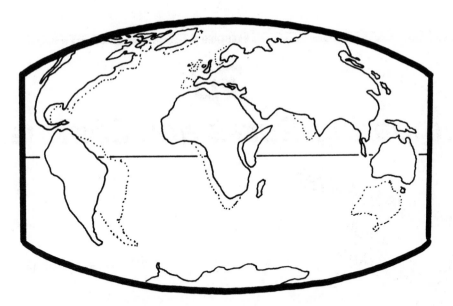

Fig. 29-7. *The continents are still drifting and a map might look like the above 50 million years from now.*

30
Comparing Rocks and Continents

Look at the eastern part of South America and notice the area that fits into the similar area of Africa (Fig. 30-1). Geologists who study the ages of rocks on both sides of the Atlantic have discovered rock formations on the western bulge of Africa that match formations that were found on South America. The two rock formations, one 2000 million years old, the other 600 million years old, are shown in Fig. 30-2. Similar matches are found between northwest Africa, North America, and western Europe (Fig. 30-3).

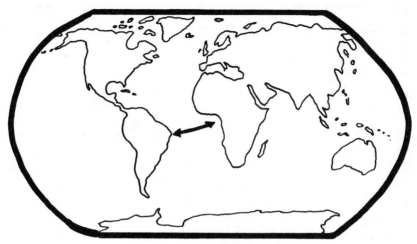

Fig. 30-1. *The east side of South America fits into the west side of Africa.*

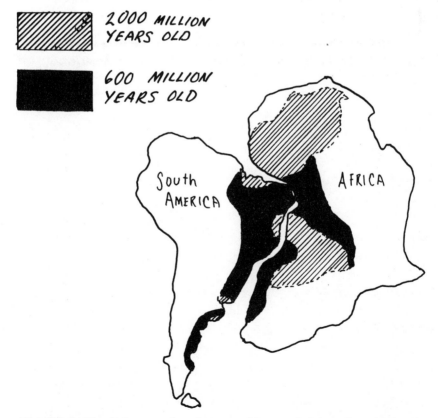

Fig. 30-2. *Shaded areas showing matching rock formations in South America and Africa.*

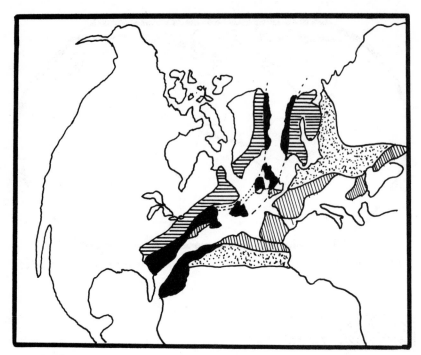

Fig. 30-3. *Matching rock formations found in North America, Africa, and Europe.*

31
Continents

Look at the map and find the seven continents (Fig. 31-1); North America, South America, Africa, Europe, Asia, Australia, and Antarctica. Except Europe and Asia, the continents are separated by bodies of water. Place the tracing paper over the map and draw the outlines of each continent. Cut out the continents (Fig. 31-2) and place them on one side of the map. You can see that only a little more than one-fourth of the earth's surface is covered by land (Fig. 31-3), about 57 million square miles, rising to an average height of about one half mile above sea level.

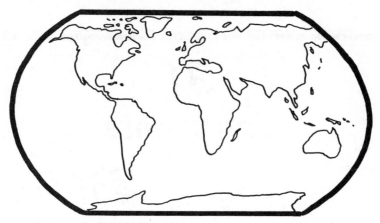

Fig. 31-1. *Map of the world showing the continents.*

Fig. 31-2. *Cut out the continents on the tracing paper.*

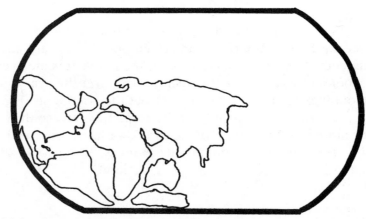

Fig. 31-3. *About one-fourth of the earth's surface is covered by land.*

32

Oceans, Islands, Peninsulas, and Isthmuses

Materials

- WORLD MAP OR GLOBE
- LARGE PAN
- SAND
- 2 ROCKS
- WATER

Look at the map and you will see that most of the earth is covered by water—almost three-fourths of the earth's surface, or more than 140 million square miles, with an average depth of about 2½ miles. The Pacific Ocean covers almost half the earth's surface (Fig. 32-1).

Pour the sand in the pan, and arrange the rocks and sand in the form of a landscape (Fig. 32-2). Slowly add the water until it surrounds the landscape (Fig. 32-3). You probably formed an island. You also may have made a peninsula, or an isthmus. An *island* is land surrounded by water. It can be in the middle of a river, lake, or an ocean. The state of Hawaii is made up of eight main islands and a number of smaller ones (Fig. 32-4). A *peninsula* is similar to an island except it is connected at one end to a larger land form. The state of Florida is a peninsula (Fig. 32-5). An *isthmus* joins two larger pieces of land. Panama is an isthmus that joins North America and South America (Fig. 32-6).

Fig. 32-1. *The Pacific Ocean covers almost half of the earth's surface.*

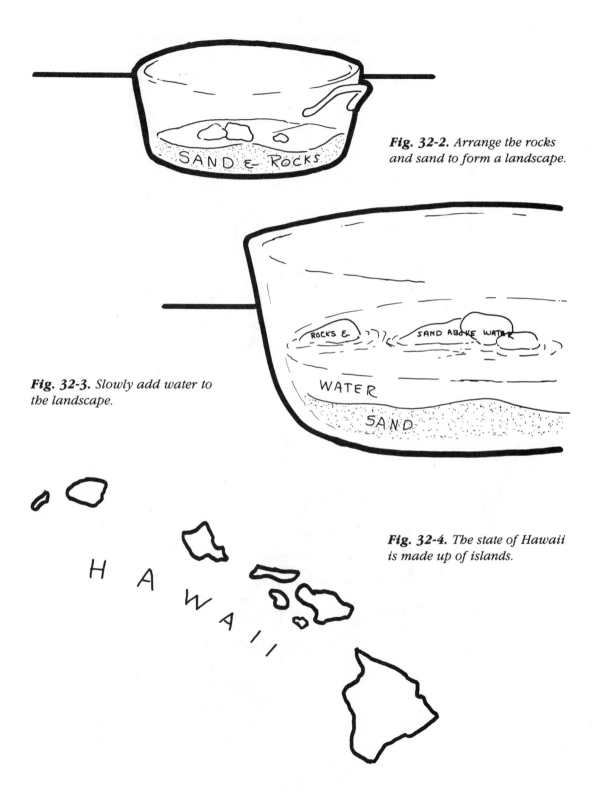

Fig. 32-2. *Arrange the rocks and sand to form a landscape.*

Fig. 32-3. *Slowly add water to the landscape.*

Fig. 32-4. *The state of Hawaii is made up of islands.*

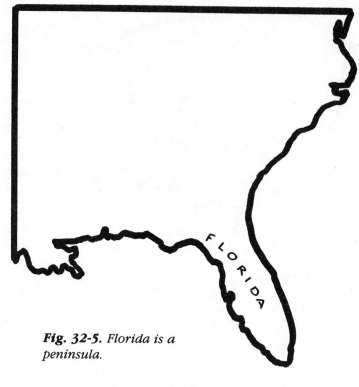

Fig. 32-5. *Florida is a peninsula.*

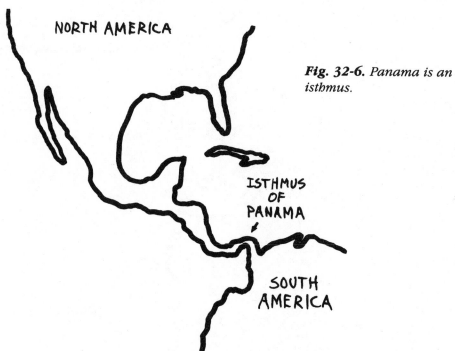

NORTH AMERICA

Fig. 32-6. *Panama is an isthmus.*

ISTHMUS
OF
PANAMA

SOUTH
AMERICA

33
Erosion

Adjust the nozzle to a fine spray similar to rainfall, and spray the bare soil a few minutes (Fig. 33-1). Soon, gullies will form, and the soil will begin to wash away. Spray the grassy area for about the same amount of time (Fig. 33-2). You will see very little of the soil washing away. The blades of grass soften the force of the rain and the roots hold the soil together. Wind and water wear away the earth in the form of erosion (Fig. 33-3). The steeper the slope of the land, the faster the water flows (Fig. 33-4). The faster the water flows, the more material it carries away. Over long periods, valleys form and grow wider. Eventually, after millions of years, the land could be almost level (Fig. 33-5).

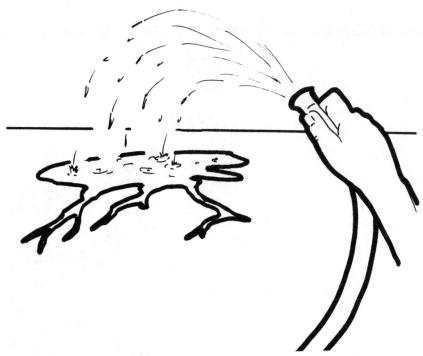

Fig. 33-1. *Spray water on the bare soil.*

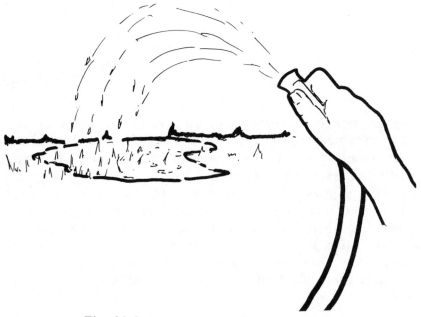

Fig. 33-2. *Spray water on the grassy area.*

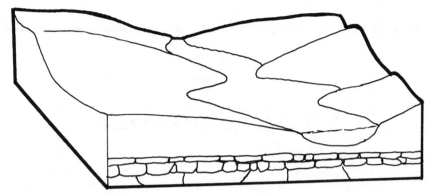

Fig. 33-3. *Erosion is caused by wind and water.*

Fig. 33-4. *Steeper slopes have greater erosion.*

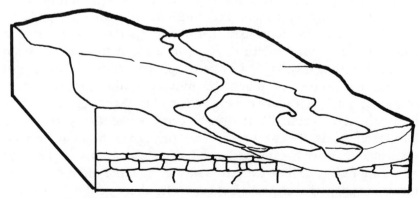

Fig. 33-5. *Eventually the land may be almost level.*

34
Soil Distribution

Materials

- SOIL
- CLEAR GLASS JAR WITH LID
- WATER

Fill the jar approximately half full of soil (Fig. 34-1), then fill it the rest of the way up with water (Fig. 34-2). Replace the lid (Fig. 34-3), and shake the jar vigorously. Let the jar stand a few days to completely settle the mixture. You will see that the soil has been separated into layers (Fig. 34-4). Moving water is one of the major causes of soil erosion. When the moving water slows down, it drops the material it was carrying. The soil is distributed according to weight. The material that streams carry is eventually deposited into lower levels of land such as lakes or oceans. Some material is deposited in the stream bed itself. This causes rivers like the Mississippi River to have muddy bottoms. Material often flows into lower fan-shaped areas called *deltas*. The delta of the Mississippi

River contains thousands of acres of fertile soil (Fig. 34-5). Sometimes rivers overflow their banks, and leave sediments when the water drains away. These areas are called *flood plains*. The soil in flood plains is normally rich because most of the sediment is made up of topsoil.

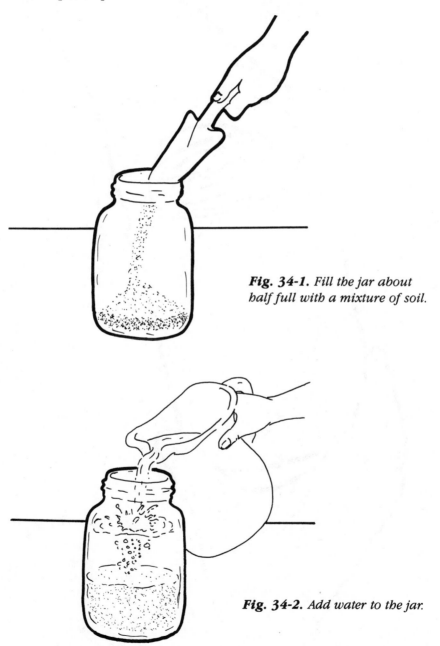

Fig. 34-1. *Fill the jar about half full with a mixture of soil.*

Fig. 34-2. *Add water to the jar.*

Fig. 34-3. _Shake the jar vigorously._

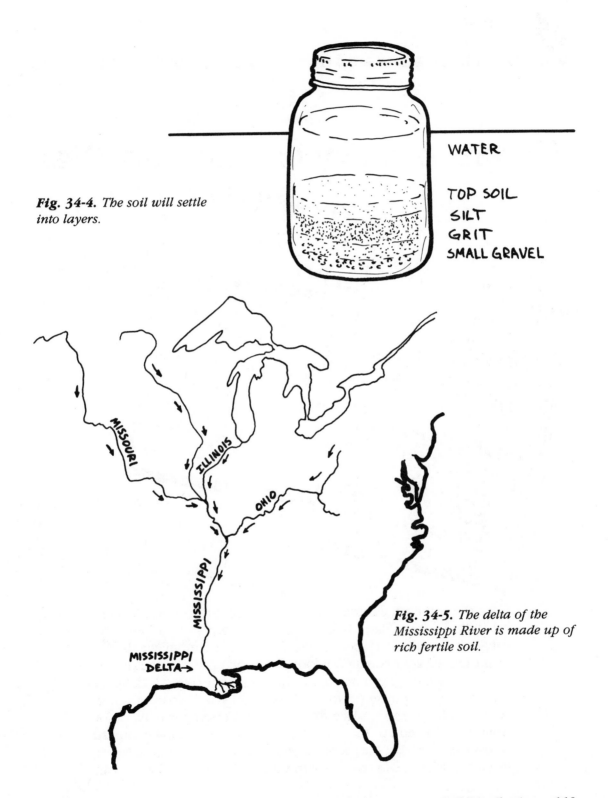

Fig. 34-4. *The soil will settle into layers.*

WATER

TOP SOIL
SILT
GRIT
SMALL GRAVEL

MISSOURI

ILLINOIS

OHIO

MISSISSIPPI

MISSISSIPPI
DELTA→

Fig. 34-5. *The delta of the Mississippi River is made up of rich fertile soil.*

35
Oceans and Population Densities

Materials

- TABLE
- BAKING PAN (ABOUT 2 INCHES DEEP)
- THERMOMETER
- WIRE CLOTHES HANGER
- RUBBER BAND
- ELECTRIC FAN
- WATER (AT

Materials

ROOM TEMPERATURE)

Place the pan on the middle of the table and fill it approximately half full of water (Fig. 35-1). Ask an adult to help you bend the hanger into a stand for the thermometer. The thermometer should be positioned approximately a foot above the table. Use the rubber band to fasten the thermometer to the wire frame (Fig. 35-2). Stand the frame approximately a foot from one end of the pan of water. With an adult present, place the electric fan approximately a foot from the other end of the pan. You want the fan to blow a breeze across the water past the thermometer (Fig. 35-3). Be careful. Never let electricity come in contact with water. Electricity and water can be very dangerous, so keep the fan away from the water. Turn on the fan and monitor the temperature. It should start to drop.

Land near the ocean during the day warms the air above it. This warm air rises and draws in the cooler air from the sea (Fig. 35-4). At night, the pattern reverses. The sea is warmer. The air above it rises and draws the cooler air out from the land (Fig. 35-5). Oceans absorb large amounts of solar energy. Because of their large capacity, their temperature rises very little during the day, and the stored energy is released slowly during the night. This equalizing effect can be seen in the difference between coastal climates and inland climates. Coastal areas normally have moderate summers and warm winters, whereas inland areas of large continents, far from the balancing effect of the ocean, have hot summers and cold winters. The oceans are important in the development of our population because all forms of life are sensitive to variations of temperatures and climate.

Fig. 35-1. *Pour water into the baking pan.*

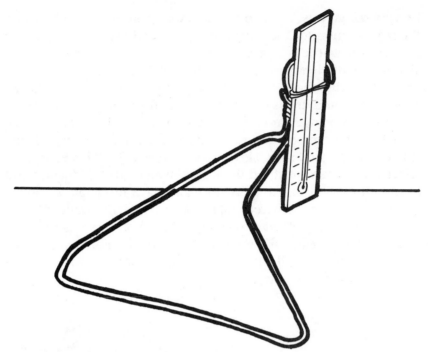

Fig. 35-2. *Attach the thermometer to the clothes hanger.*

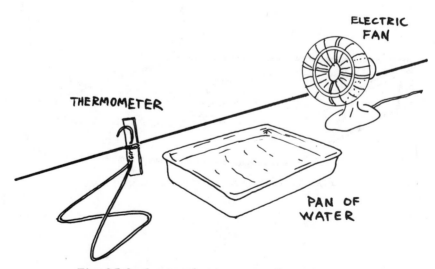

Fig. 35-3. *Create a breeze across the water.*

Fig. 35-4. *During the day cooler air is drawn in from the sea.*

Fig. 35-5. *At night cooler air is drawn out from the land.*

36
Tropical Rain Forests

Place one hand on top of the globe and slowly turn it to the right, or counterclockwise looking down at the North Pole (Fig. 36-1). This is the same direction that the earth spins. As the globe turns, draw a chalk line straight down from the North Pole to the equator (Fig. 36-2). Stop the globe and examine the chalk line. It should not be a straight line, but a curved one that approaches the equator at an angle. The line should run from the northeast toward the southwest. The warm air near the equator rises and draws the cooler air in from the poles. Air moves from the poles to the equator and back to the poles in a continuous cycle (Fig. 36-3). Because of the earth's rotation, air currents tend to curve to the right of the direction they are traveling in the Northern Hemisphere, and curve to the left in the

Southern Hemisphere. These winds are called the *trade winds* (Fig. 36-4). Because of these winds and the locations of the tropical rain forests, scientists have discovered a connection between the rain forests and climate around the world. The rain forests are found in the area between 23.5 degrees north latitude and 23.5 degrees south latitude (Fig. 36-5). Studies have shown that when a rain forest is destroyed, it could take 1000 years for new growth to be established.

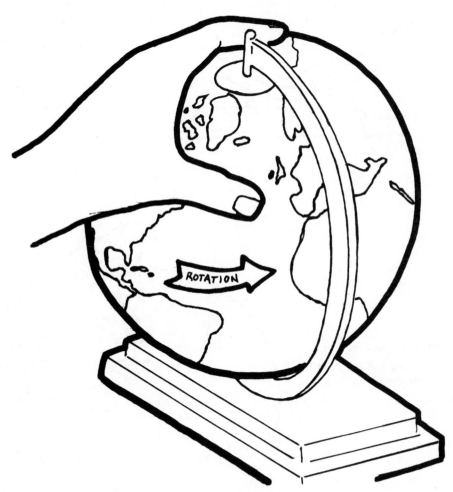

Fig. 36-1. *Rotate the globe to the right.*

Fig. 36-2. Draw a chalk line down toward the equator.

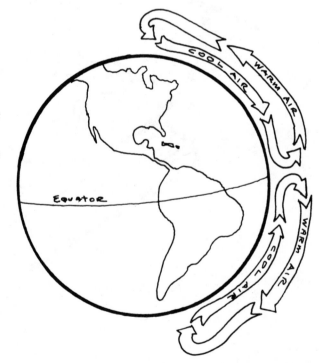

Fig. 36-3. Air moves continuously from the poles to the equator and back to the poles.

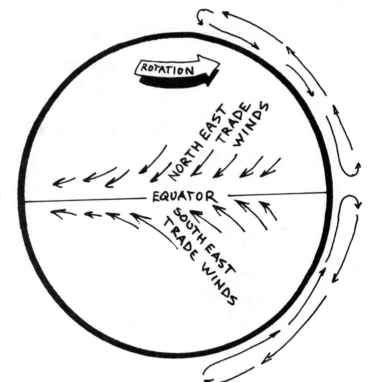

Fig. 36-4. *The rotation of the earth creates the trade winds.*

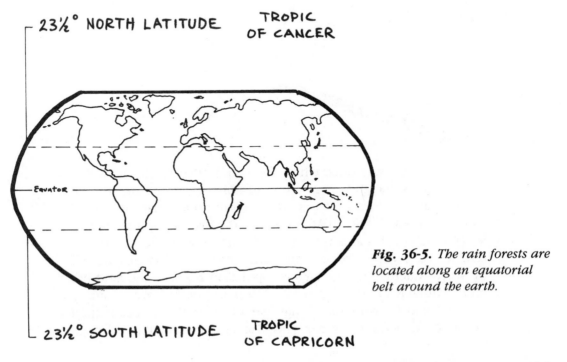

23½° NORTH LATITUDE — TROPIC OF CANCER

Fig. 36-5. *The rain forests are located along an equatorial belt around the earth.*

23½° SOUTH LATITUDE — TROPIC OF CAPRICORN

37

Land Use
and Population Densities

Materials

MAP OF NORTH
AMERICA

Study the map and notice where the major cities are located. You can see that some areas have a number of cities close together. In other areas the cities are far apart. You will notice that the central and western part of North America have the lowest population (Fig. 37-1). Much of this area is made up of high plains and deserts, or remote areas with extreme temperature changes. The eastern half of North America has the larger population because the land has more natural resources (Fig. 37-2). *Natural resources* are resources that provide us with the things we need to live. Most natural resources depend on water and the annual rainfall. Although coastal areas along the northwest receive large amounts of rain, the wettest areas are in the southeast. This provides a rich agriculture region with access to sea ports for shipping.

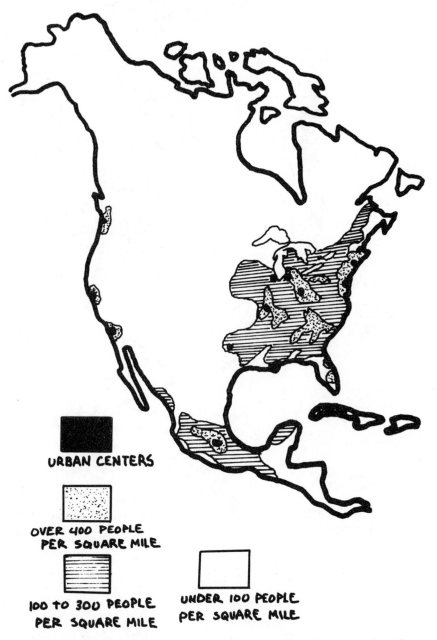

URBAN CENTERS

OVER 400 PEOPLE PER SQUARE MILE

100 TO 300 PEOPLE PER SQUARE MILE

UNDER 100 PEOPLE PER SQUARE MILE

Fig. 37-1. *The central and western part of North America has the lowest population.*

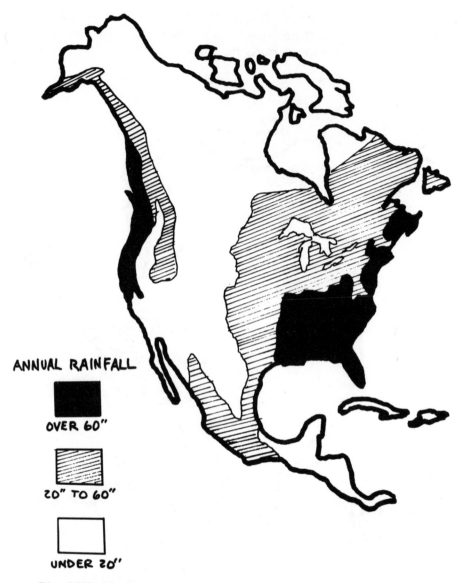

ANNUAL RAINFALL

OVER 60"

20" TO 60"

UNDER 20"

Fig. 37-2. *The largest population is located in the eastern half of North America.*

38
Inland Waterways
and Population Densities

Look at the map and study the eastern part of the United States. In Fig. 38-1, notice that a waterway runs from Lake Michigan to the Gulf of Mexico. An *inland waterway* is a canal, lake, or river that is deep and wide enough to be used by boats and barges. The standard depth for most inland shipping channels is nine feet. Inland waterways provide important shipping routes for agricultural and manufacturing products (Fig. 38-2). Water transportation has always been important to the development of cities and the growth of their population. The earliest civilizations were developed along rivers (Fig. 38-3). Rivers have been the highways for logging and lumber industries for many years (Fig. 38-4). Huge dams store large volumes of water for irrigation, flood control, and electrical generating plant operations (Fig. 38-5). Where there are rivers, there is usually some form of recreation (Fig. 38-6).

Fig. 38-1. *Inland waterways in the United States.*

Fig. 38-2. *Inland waterways provide transportation for freight.*

Fig. 38-3. *Early civilizations settled along rivers.*

Fig. 38-4. *Rivers provide transportation for logging industries.*

Fig. 38-5. *Dams store water to generate electricity.*

Fig. 38-6. *Rivers and lakes provide recreation.*

39

Manufacturing and Geography

Study the map and notice that from experiments 37 and 38, we can see that the natural resources and the population are related. Manufacturing and population are also related. Manufacturing plants are important to the welfare of their communities. For example, for each 100 people who work in a factory, about 175 people are needed to provide services and goods for these workers. But only a small portion of the land is devoted to industry. Most of the land is used for farming and grazing. One of the most interesting facts about the distribution of manufacturing in the United States is the huge nonindustrial area. Large regions of the West such as the Great Plains, the Rocky Mountains, and the Sierra Nevada Mountains show a blank on the manufacturing map in Fig. 39-1. The West Coast, however, has concentrations of manufacturing around Los Angeles, San Francisco, Portland, and Seattle. Most big manufacturers are near large cities, chiefly in the northeastern area of the country. We can see that manufacturing industries are normally located in regions that have plenty of natural resources, good transportation, mild climates, and large populations.

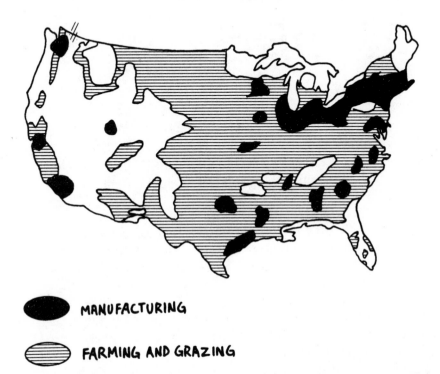

MANUFACTURING

FARMING AND GRAZING

Fig. 39-1. *Populations are greater in areas that have more natural resources.*

Science Fair Projects

A science fair project is an exciting way to learn about geography, but it will require some thought and planning (Fig. 40-1). The more planning, the better the chances of a successful project. One of the most important parts in planning a project is choosing the subject. You need to give this a lot of thought. Otherwise, you might discover later that the materials were not available, or too expensive, or that the project was just too complicated. If this happens, the project might be abandoned, and you might not have enough time to start another. Try to choose a subject you like, one you are familiar with, or one you would like to know more about. Just spend some time thinking about it, and try to keep it within your abilities. A simple project, well done, can be much more successful than a complicated one that is poorly done. Many scientific discoveries were made using simple equipment.

You might begin by dividing your science fair projects into basic steps such as: (1) choosing a topic, (2) forming questions and the hypothesis, your guess of the results of your experiment, (3) doing the experiment, and (4) recording the results and conclusions of the experiment.

A report is usually included in a science fair project (Fig. 40-2). The report should explain what you wanted to prove or answer a question that you had. Graphs and charts can be helpful in providing information about your project. Your report should include a complete description of your project, and the results and conclusions you made based on the project.

Once you have selected the topic of your project, choose a specific question to be answered or proved. Don't generalize. Have a definite problem to solve, or a point to prove. For example, if you

Fig. 40-1. *Considerable planning is important to a successful science fair project.*

Fig. 40-2. *A report will help you gather information for your project.*

were interested in early explorers, you could make a simple compass, and use a world map to show how early seafarers were limited to moving from point to point along the coasts until the 1100s. About this time, crude magnetic compasses came into use. This encouraged the sailors to sail to remote seas.

If you are interested in how mountains are formed, you could use layers of different colored clays on a sheet of stretched rubber. When the rubber is released, the layers of clay will be pushed together, and up, to form mountains. Or you could cut out patterns of the continents, and show how, at one time, they were joined together, then drifted to their present locations.

After you have selected your project, you'll want to display your experiment. You may need to build a model. Usually these can be made from wood, cardboard, or handy items that are found around the home (Fig. 40-3). Often throwaway items can be used. This could include empty coffee cans, plastic or glass bottles, cardboard tubes from paper towels or tissue paper, and wooden spools from sewing thread. By being creative, you will have a wider selection of materials.

Fig. 40-3. *You might use items found in the home to make a model.*

Your project will probably be displayed on a table. A wooden or cardboard panel can be placed behind the project. Information about your experiment can be mounted on this panel (Fig. 40-4). The panel can be in three sections. The two end panels can be angled forward so that the project can stand by itself, like the back of a theater stage. The left side of the panel might show the purpose of your experiment—why you chose the topic or what you wanted to prove. The center panel can show how your experiment was constructed, and the right panel can show the results of your experiment. This also can include the conclusions that you've made, along with possible uses for this information.

By planning and using your imagination, you can expand and develop a simple experiment into an interesting and educational one. Most experiments will have been done before, but maybe your experiment will uncover something new. You might have approached the topic with a different point of view. Geography

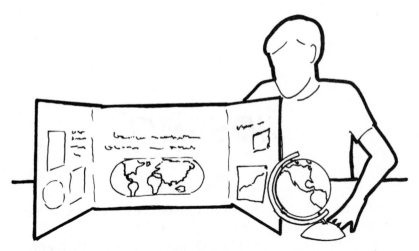

Fig. 40-4. *A panel can display information about your project.*

depends on information from other fields such as geology, mathematics, physics, astronomy, meteorology, and biology. Geography is an old science, but with new information being gathered everyday, new discoveries are bound to happen in the study of people and their environment.

Glossary

asthenosphere   A molten area inside the earth, between the lithosphere and the mantle.

average   The result obtained by dividing a sum by the number of quantities added; pertaining to the usual or ordinary kind.

continental drift   The theory that continents slowly shift their positions as a result of currents in the molten rocks beneath the earth's crust.

continents   The largest land masses on earth; Africa, Antarctica, Asia, Australia, Europe, North America, and South America.

contour line   An imaginary line that connects points on the ground with the same elevation above a reference plane.

core   The center of the earth, including the inner core, which is solid, and the outer core, which is liquid.

delta   A deposit of sand and soil, usually triangular, formed at the mouth of some rivers.

depression contour line   An imaginary line that connects points on the ground with the same elevation below a reference plane.

equator   An imaginary circle around the earth, equally distant at all points from both the North Pole and the South Pole; 0 degree latitude.

erosion   The wearing away of land or rock by wind or water.

fault   A break in a rock formation that is caused by shifting of the earth's crust, along which movement can occur.

flood plain   A plain along a river, formed from sediment that is deposited by floods.

Greenwich Observatory   The oldest observatory in constant use marking the prime meridian; 0 degree longitude.

Greenwich time   Solar time of the meridian of Greenwich, England, used as the basis for standard time throughout most of the world; also called *universal time* or UT.

hypothesis A possible answer to a question or solution to a problem.

islands Land that is surrounded by water.

isoline A line on a map that connects points of equal densities.

isthmus A small piece of land that connects two larger pieces.

legend A brief description, or key, that accompanies an illustration or map.

lines of latitude Lines that are drawn around the earth, parallel to the equator, on maps and globes. They are used to indicate distances and locate points on the earth's surface in relation to the equator.

lines of longitude Lines that are drawn from north to south on maps and globes to indicate distances and locate points.

lithosphere The solid outer part of the earth, including its crust, or exposed surface.

magnetic declination The difference between true north and magnetic north.

magnetic deviation The deflection of a compass needle due to outside magnetic influences.

mantle A solid part of the earth's interior, between the core and the asthenosphere.

mean Designates a figure that is intermediate between two extremes and implies moderation.

median The middle number or point in a series arranged in order of size.

meridian A great circle of the earth passing through the geographic poles and any given point on the earth's surface.

middle The point or part that is equally distant from either or all sides or extremities and may apply to space or time.

minutes The sixtieth part of any of certain units; 1/60 of a degree of an arc.

orientate To adjust to a specified direction.

peninsula Land that is similar to an island, but is connected to other land at one end.

prime meridian The meridian from which longitude is measured both east and west; 0 degree longitude. It passes through Greenwich, England.

San Andreas fault An active fault in the earth's crust extending northwest from southern California for about 600 miles.

scale of miles The proportion that a map bears to the thing that it represents; ratio between the dimensions of a representation and those of the object (a scale of 1 inch to a mile).

seconds   1/60 of a minute of angular measurement.

solar energy   Energy produced by or coming from the sun.

trade wind   A wind that blows steadily toward the equator from the northeast in the tropics north of the equator and from the southeast in the tropics south of the equator.

tropical rain forests   Dense, evergreen forests that occupy a tropical region having abundant rainfall throughout the year.